CUTE MERMAID COLORING BOOK
FOR KIDS AGES 4-8

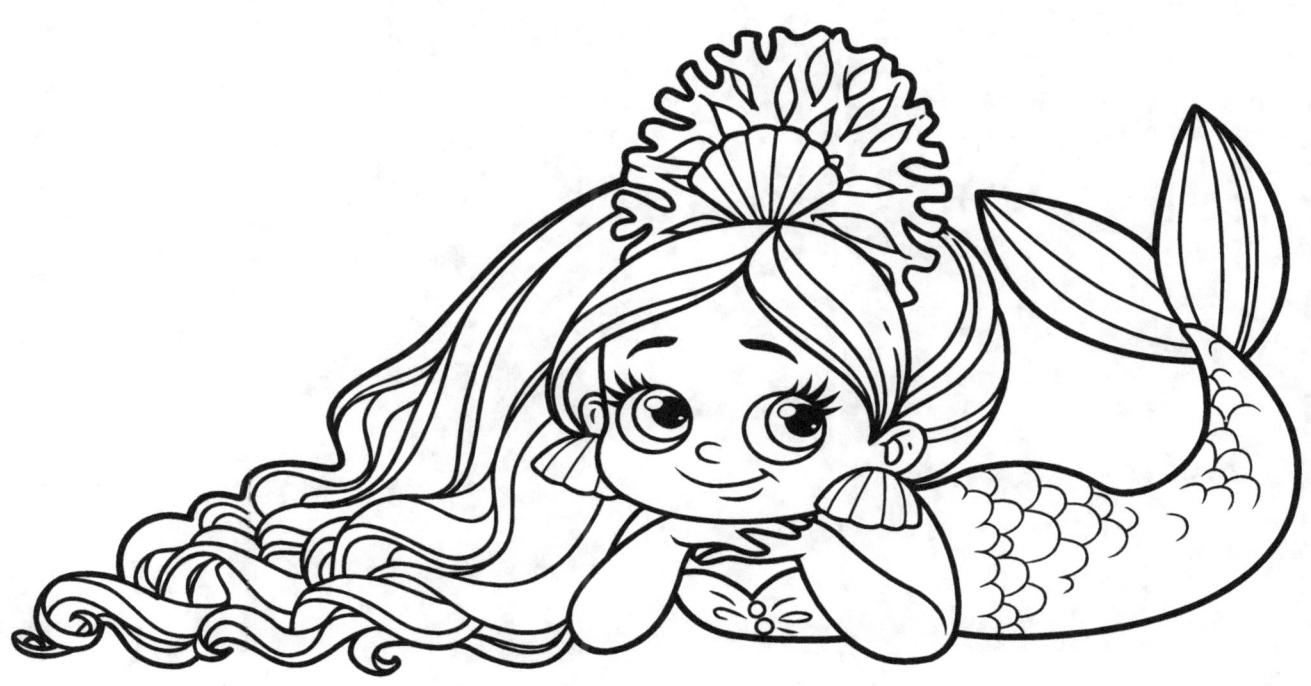

BELONGS TO

_____

Copyright @2021 by JDroy Sky Publishing

All rights reserved.

For any inquiries or questions regarding our books,
please contact us at : jdroyskypublishing@gmail.com

ISBN: 9798533339742

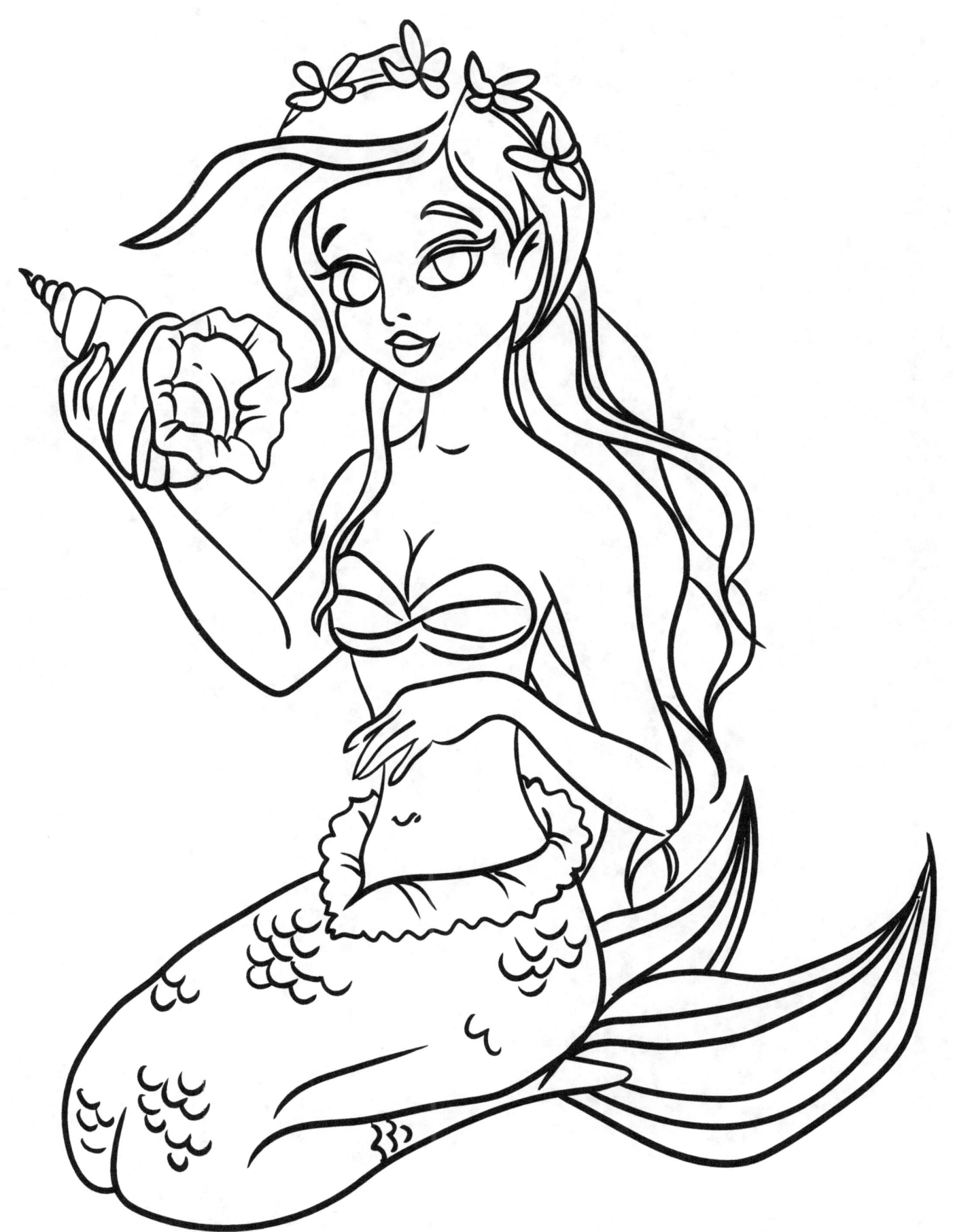

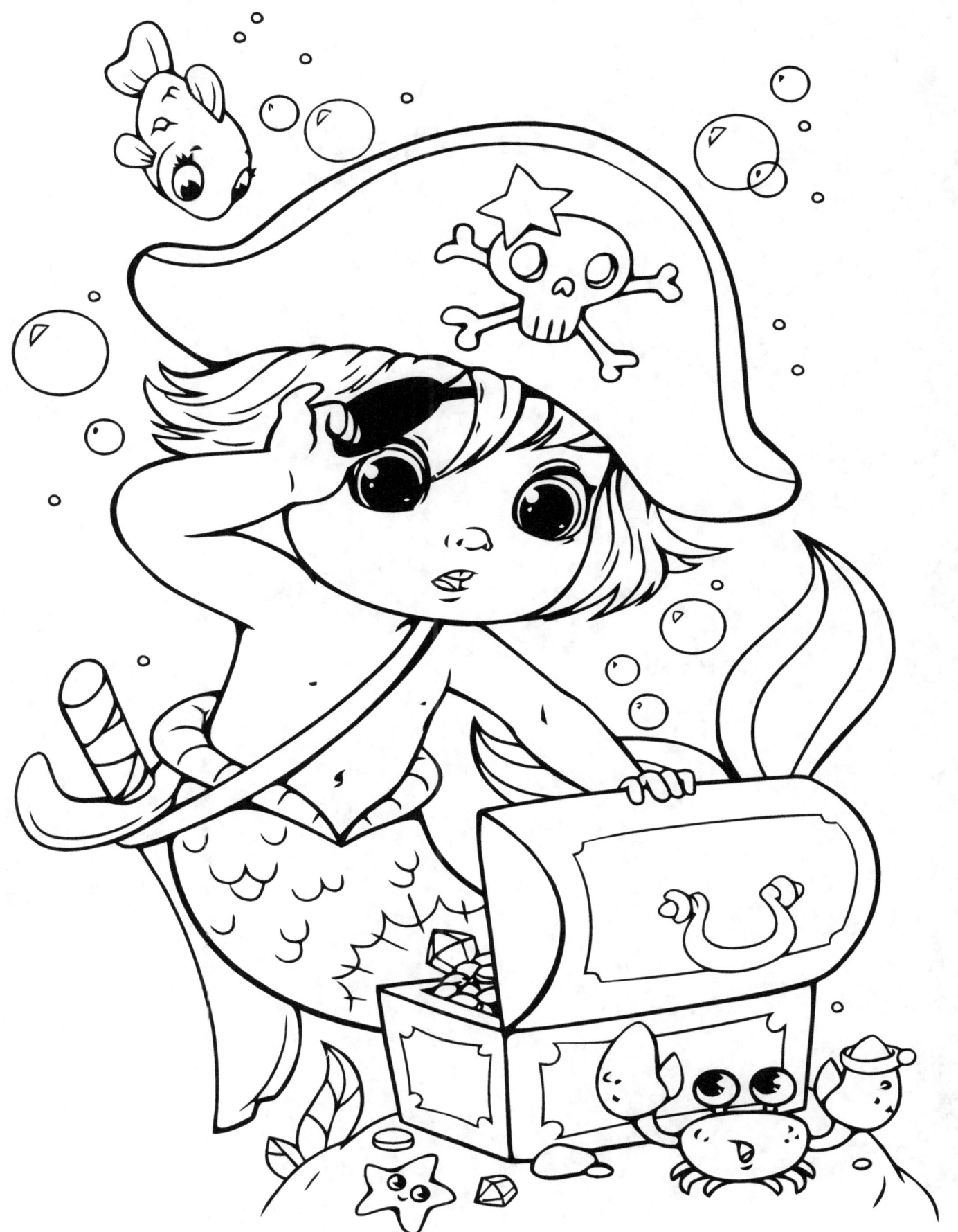

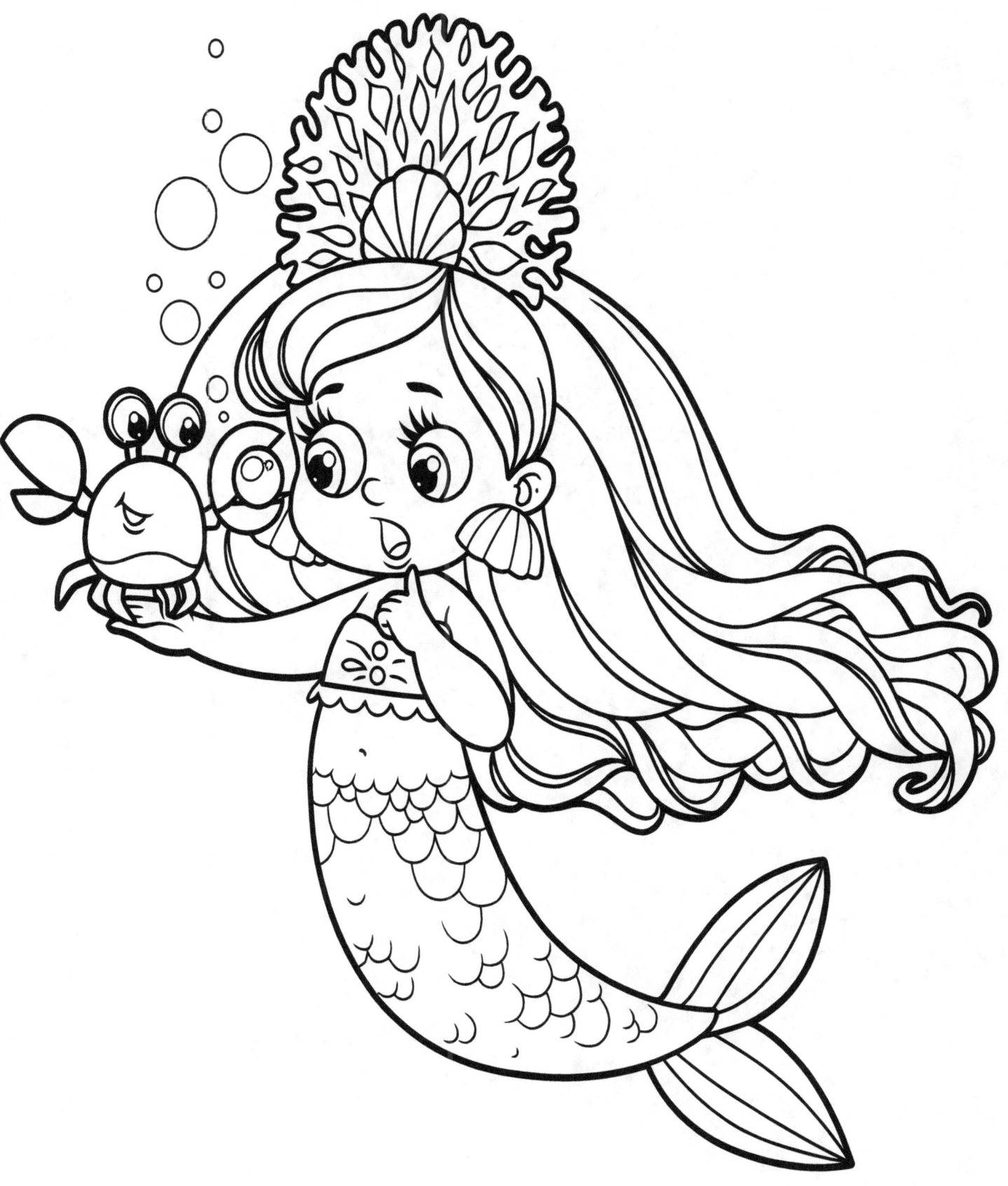

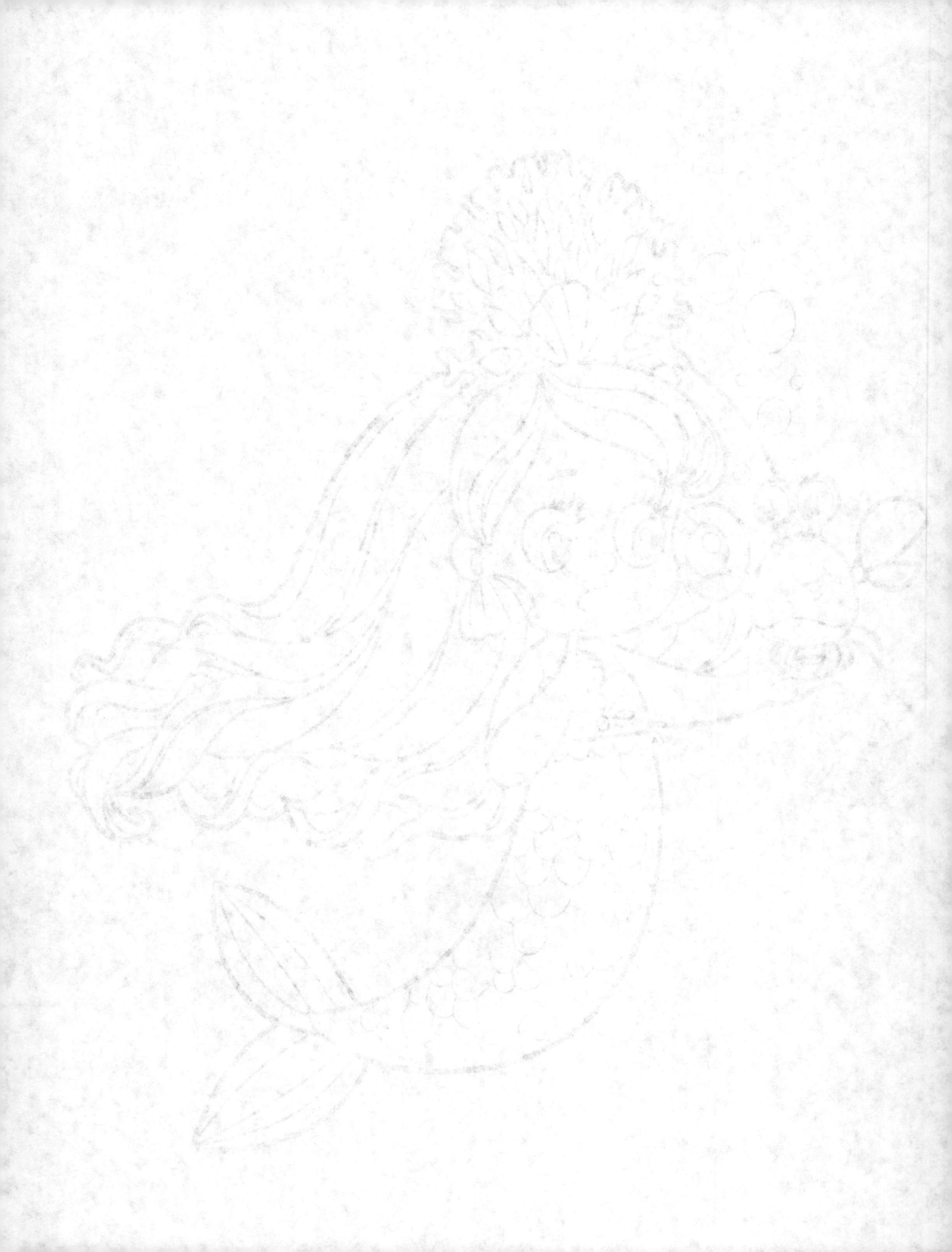

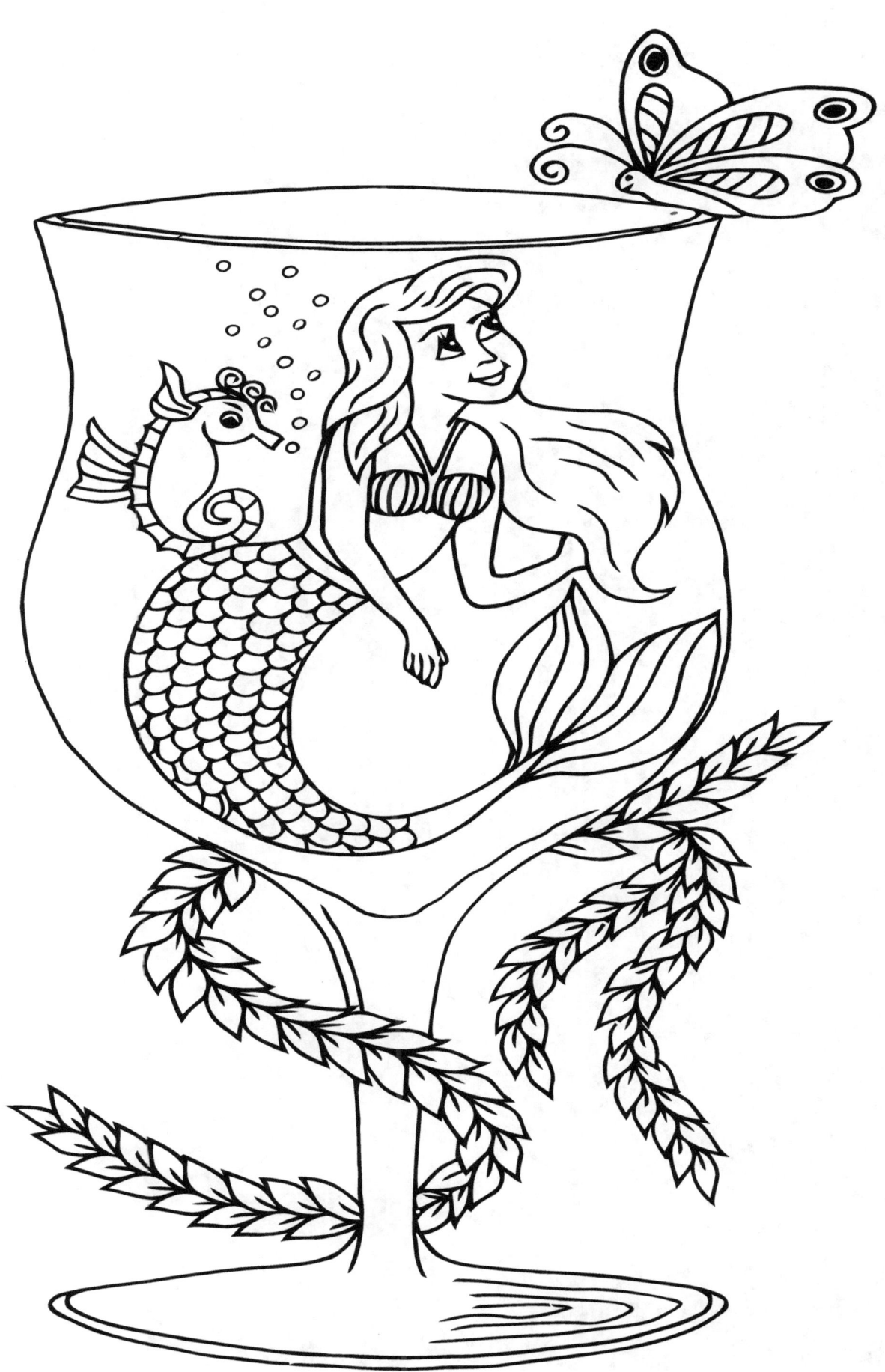

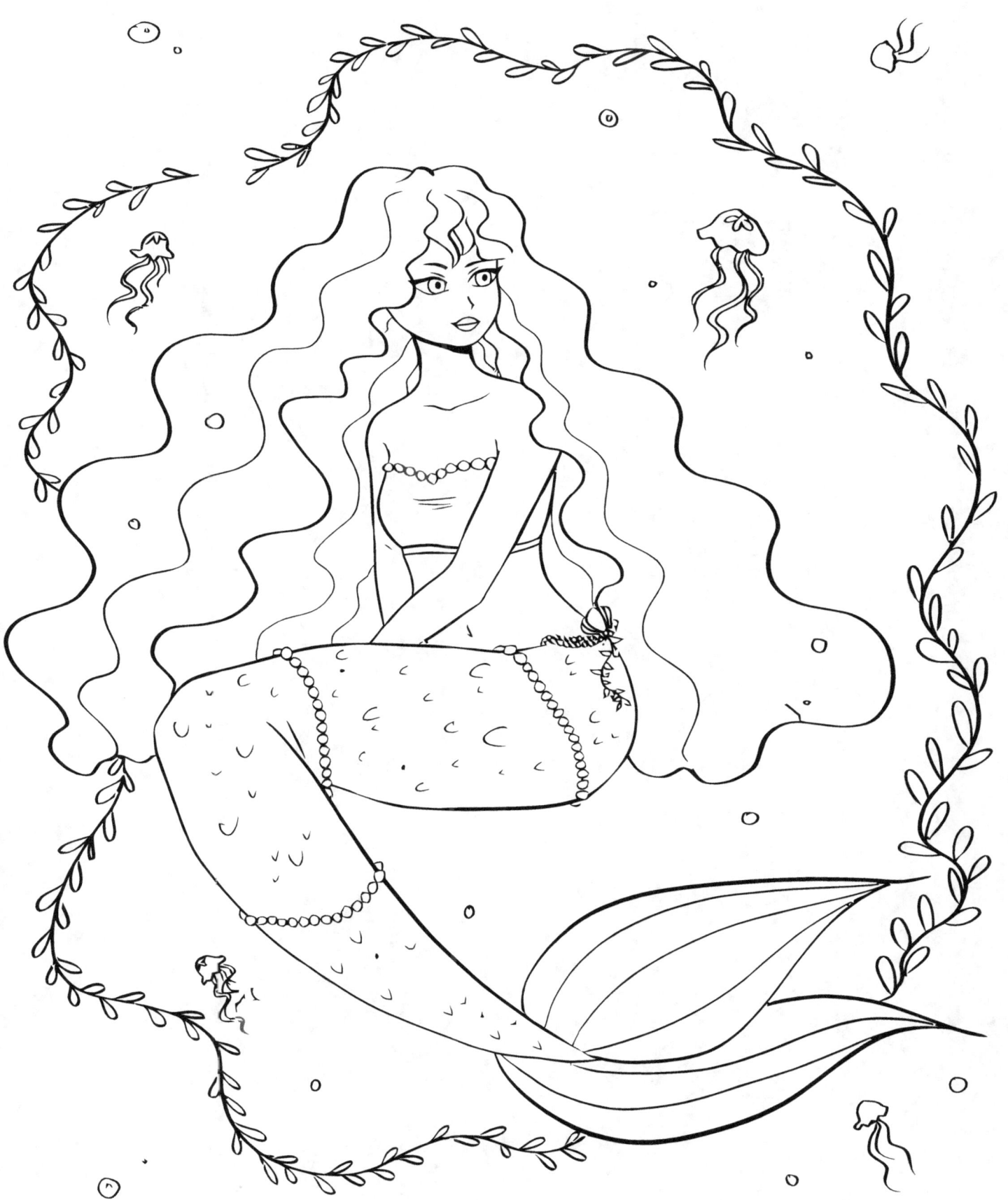

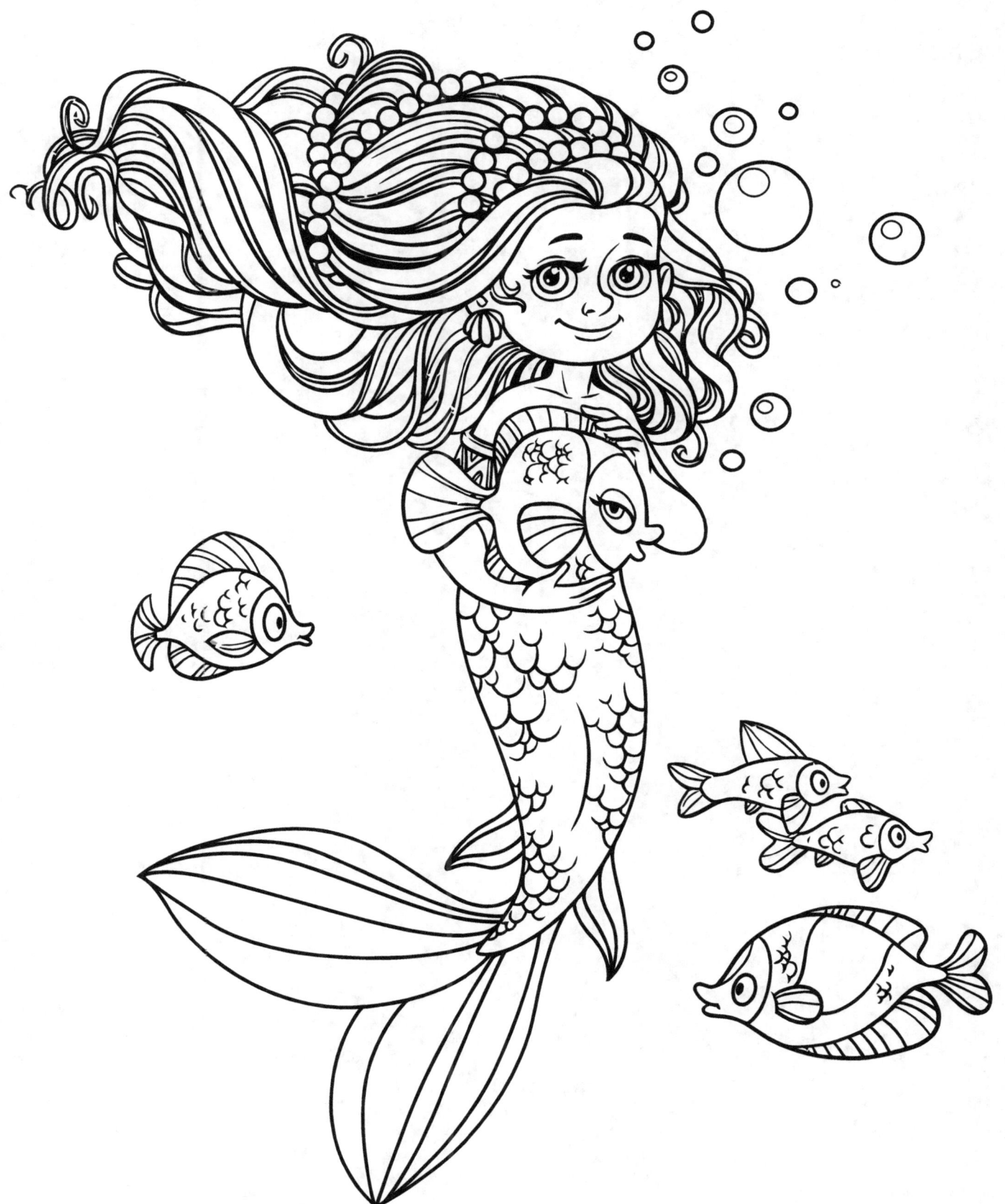

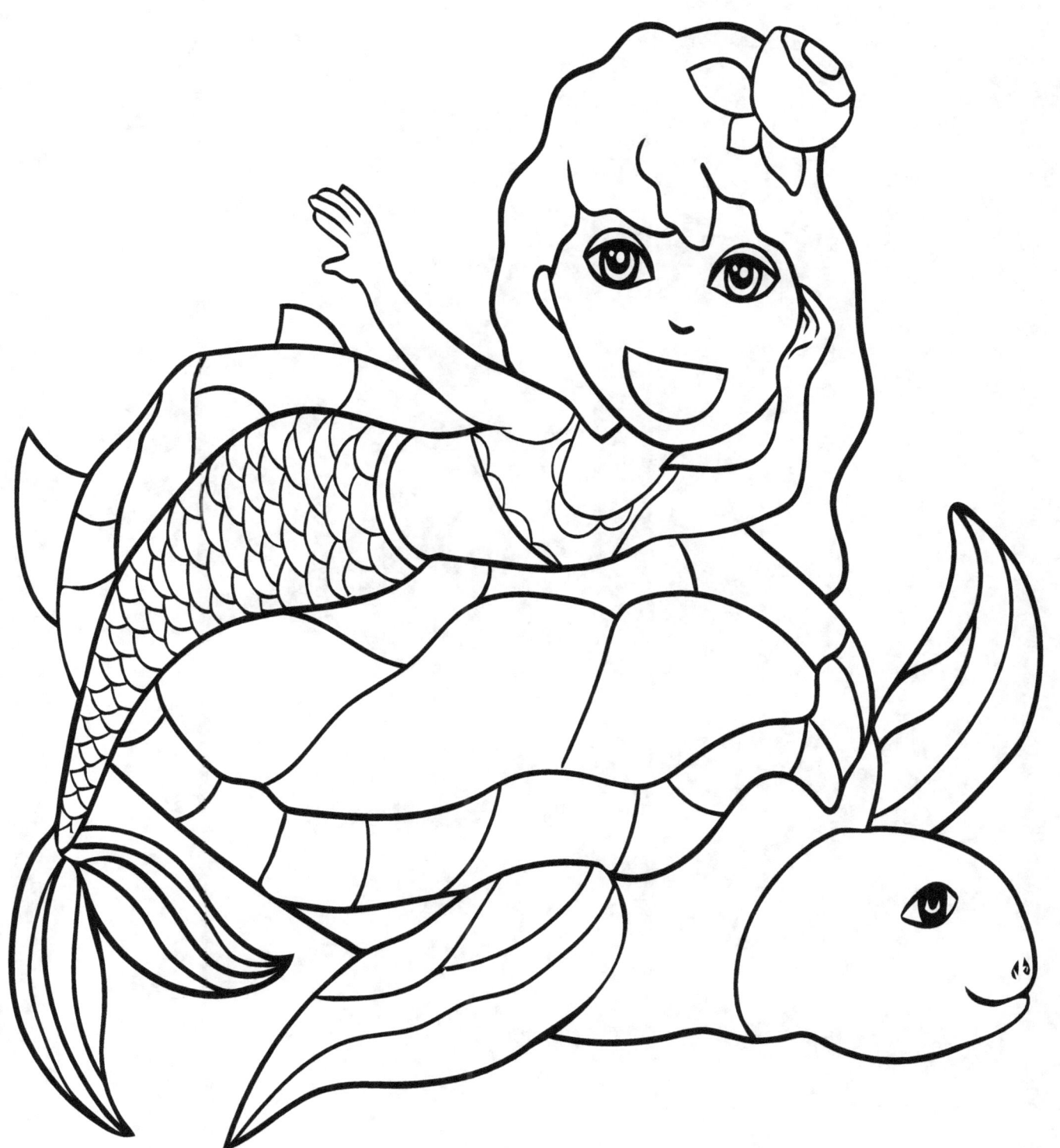

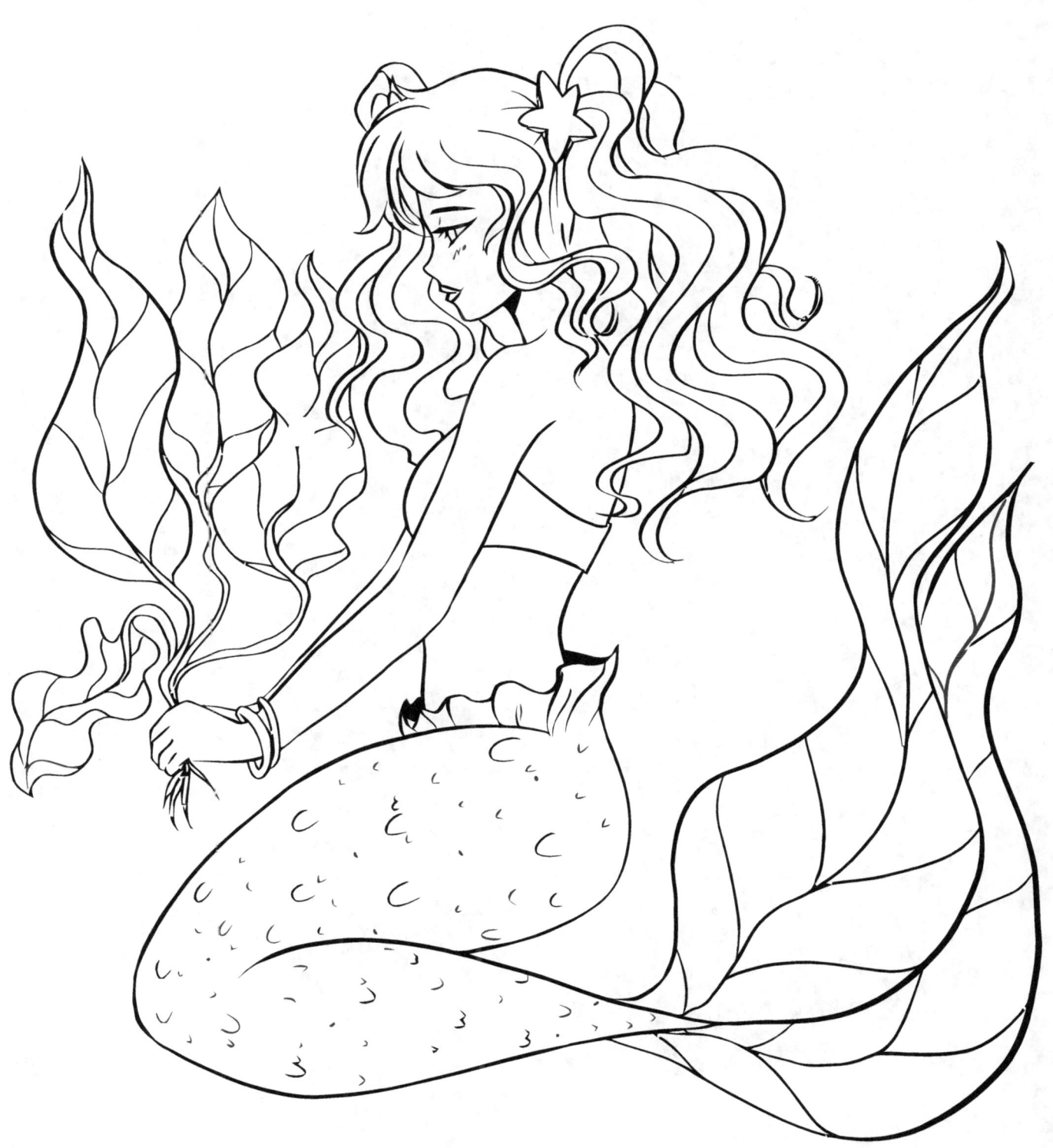

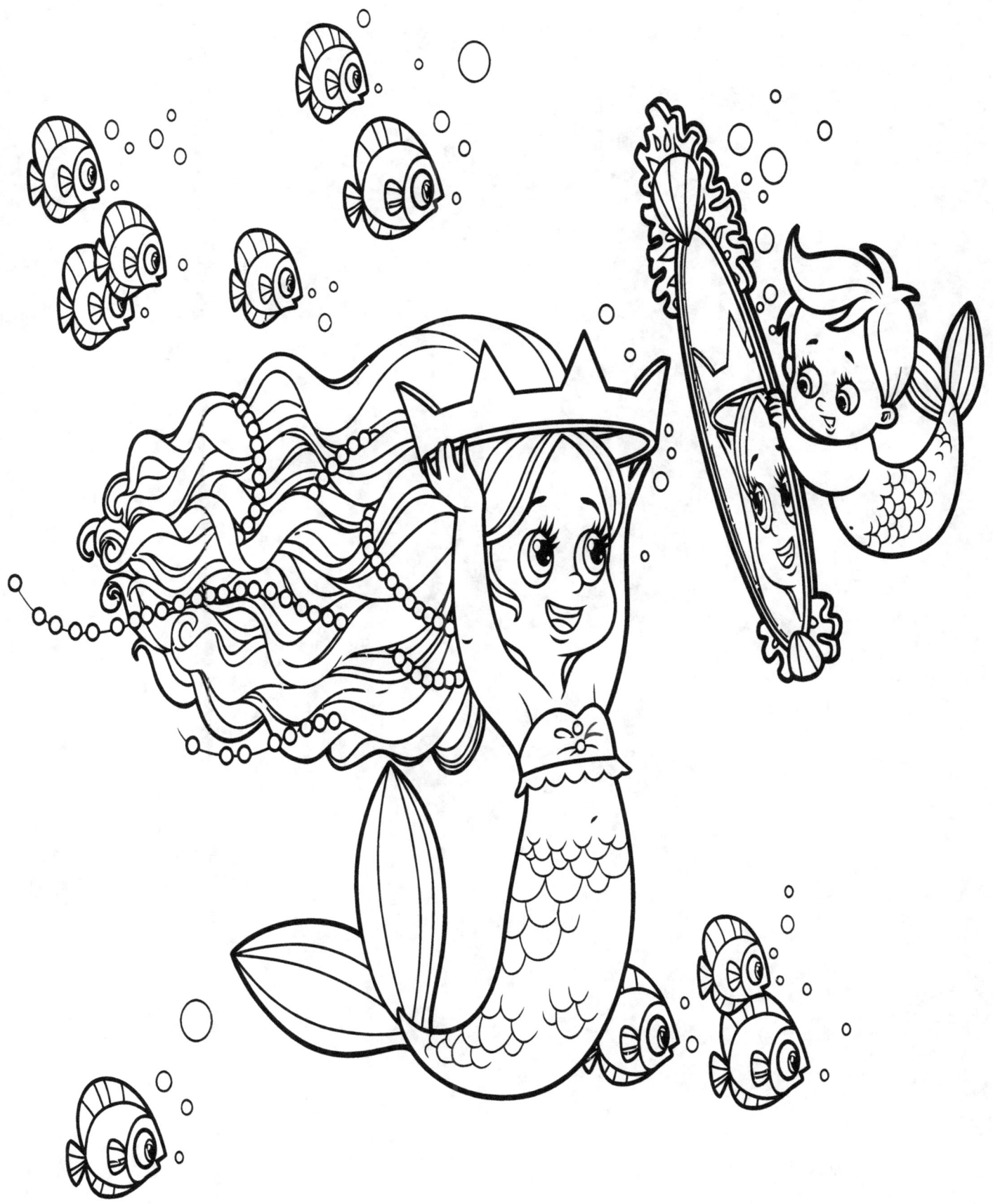

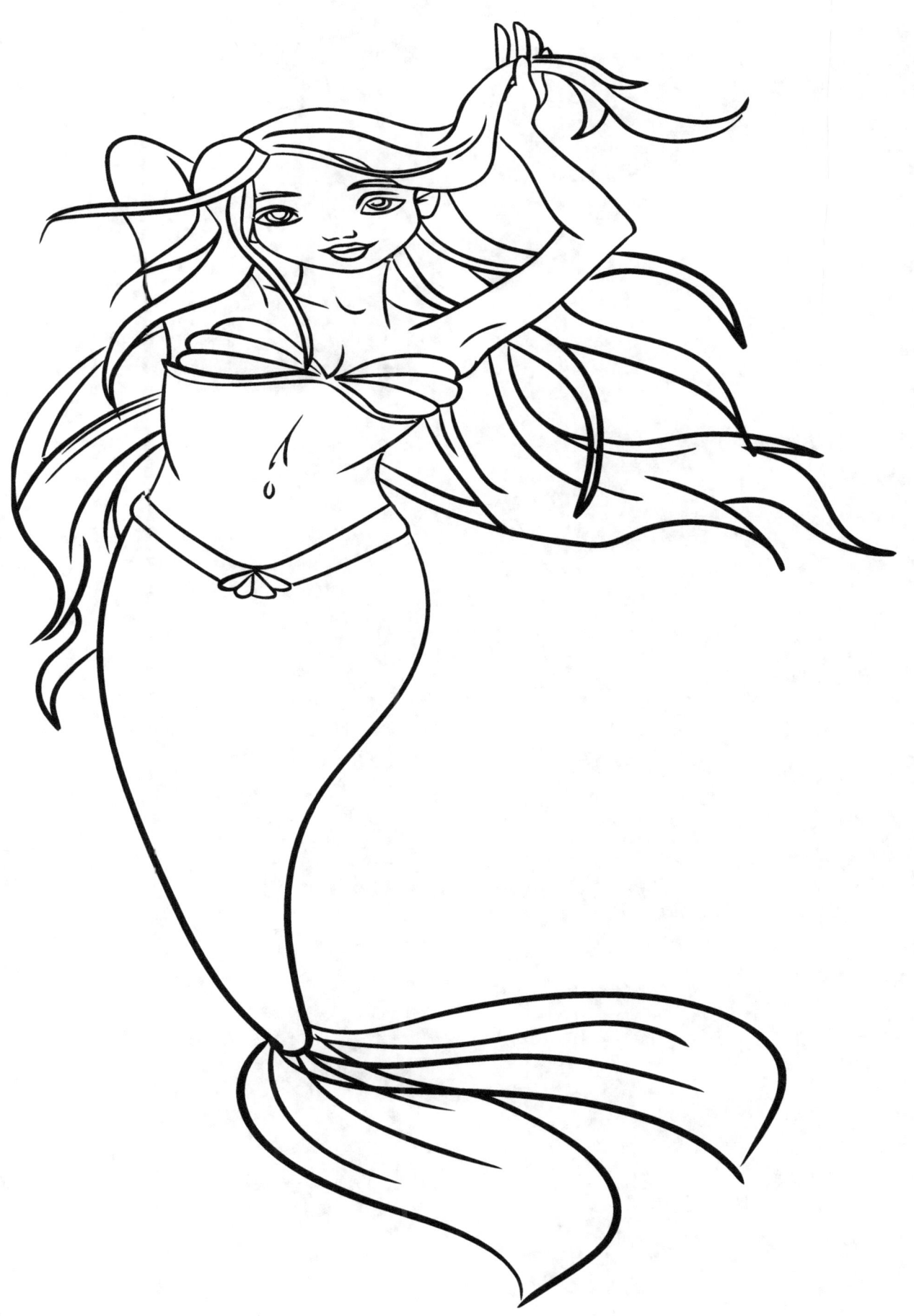

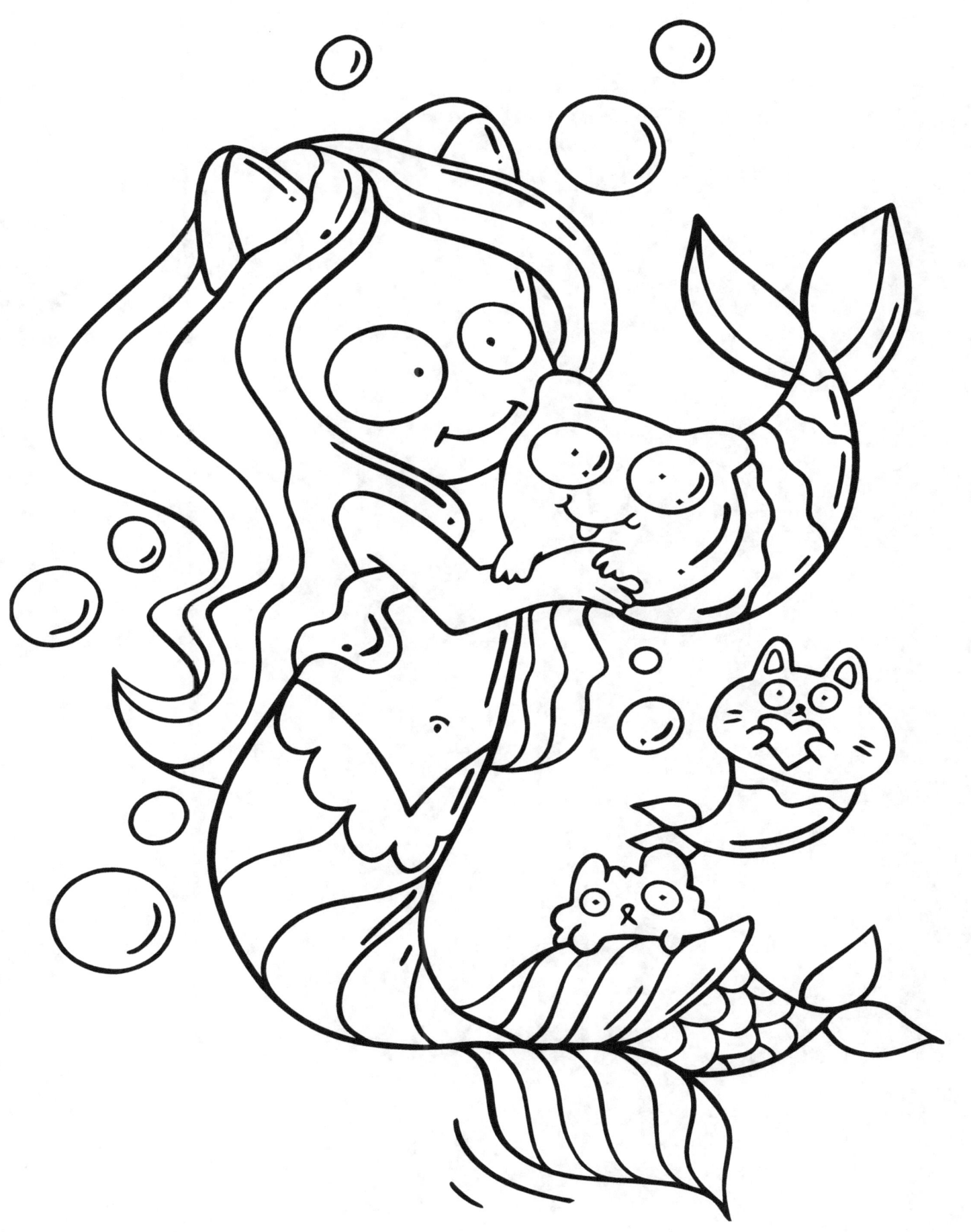

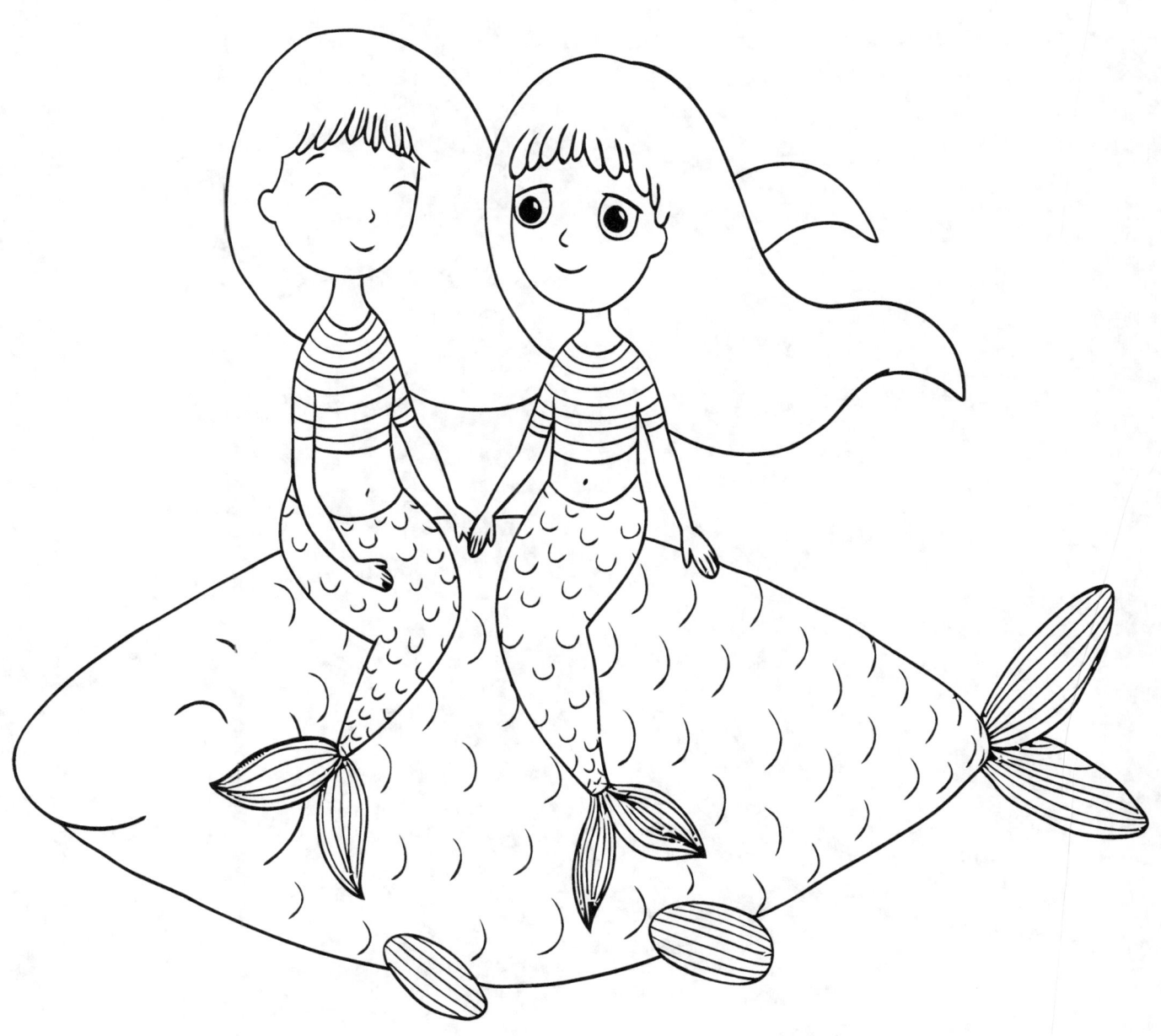

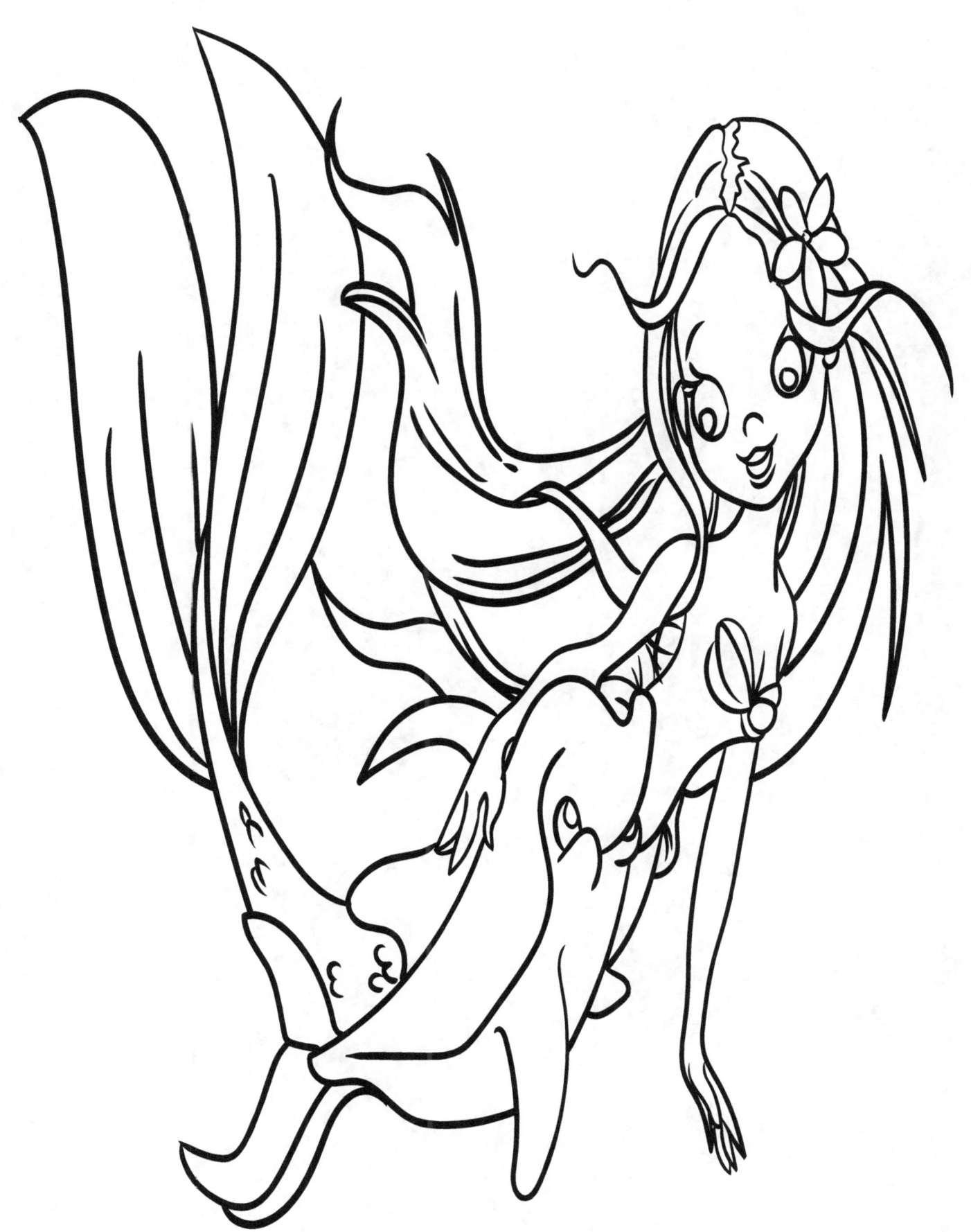

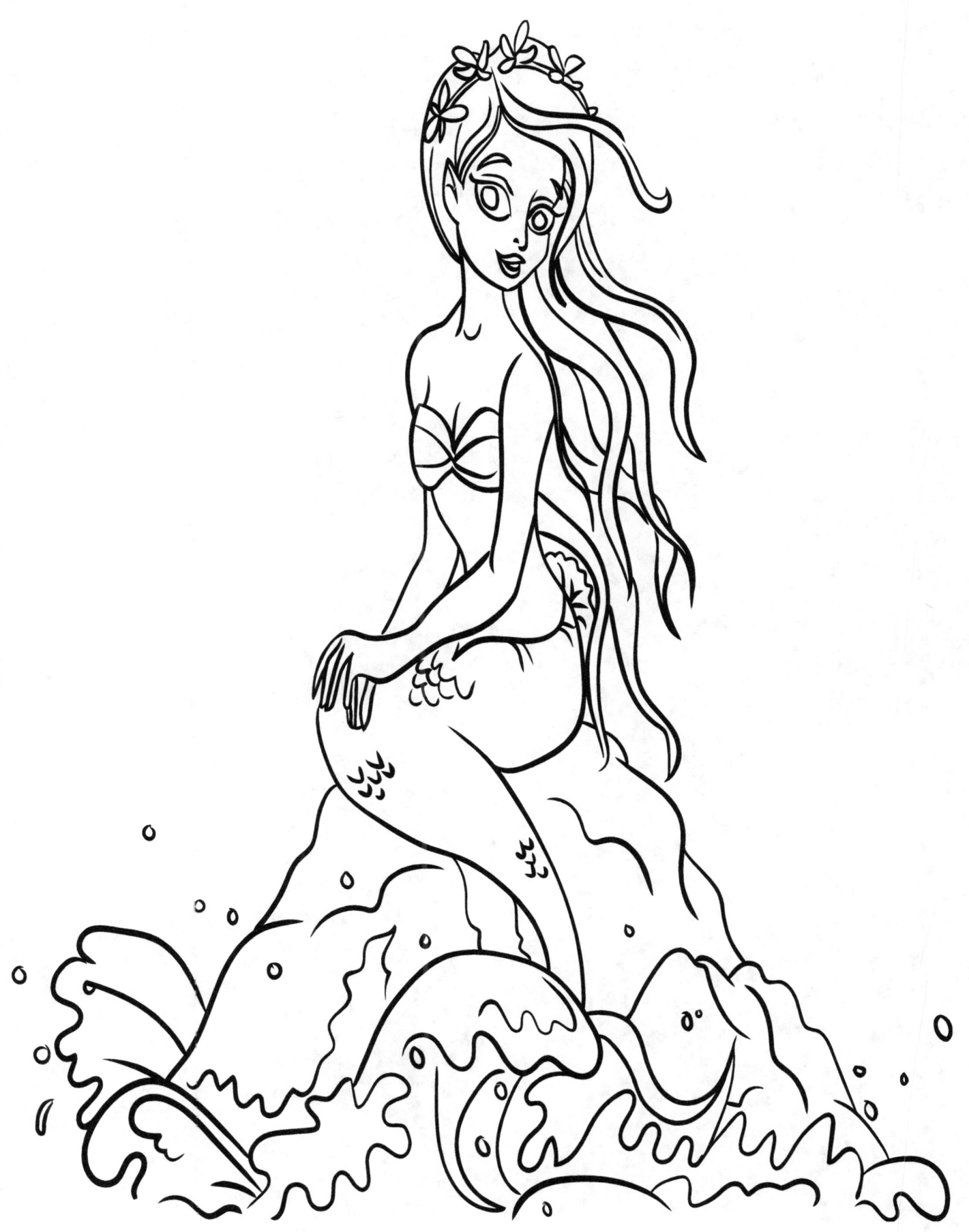

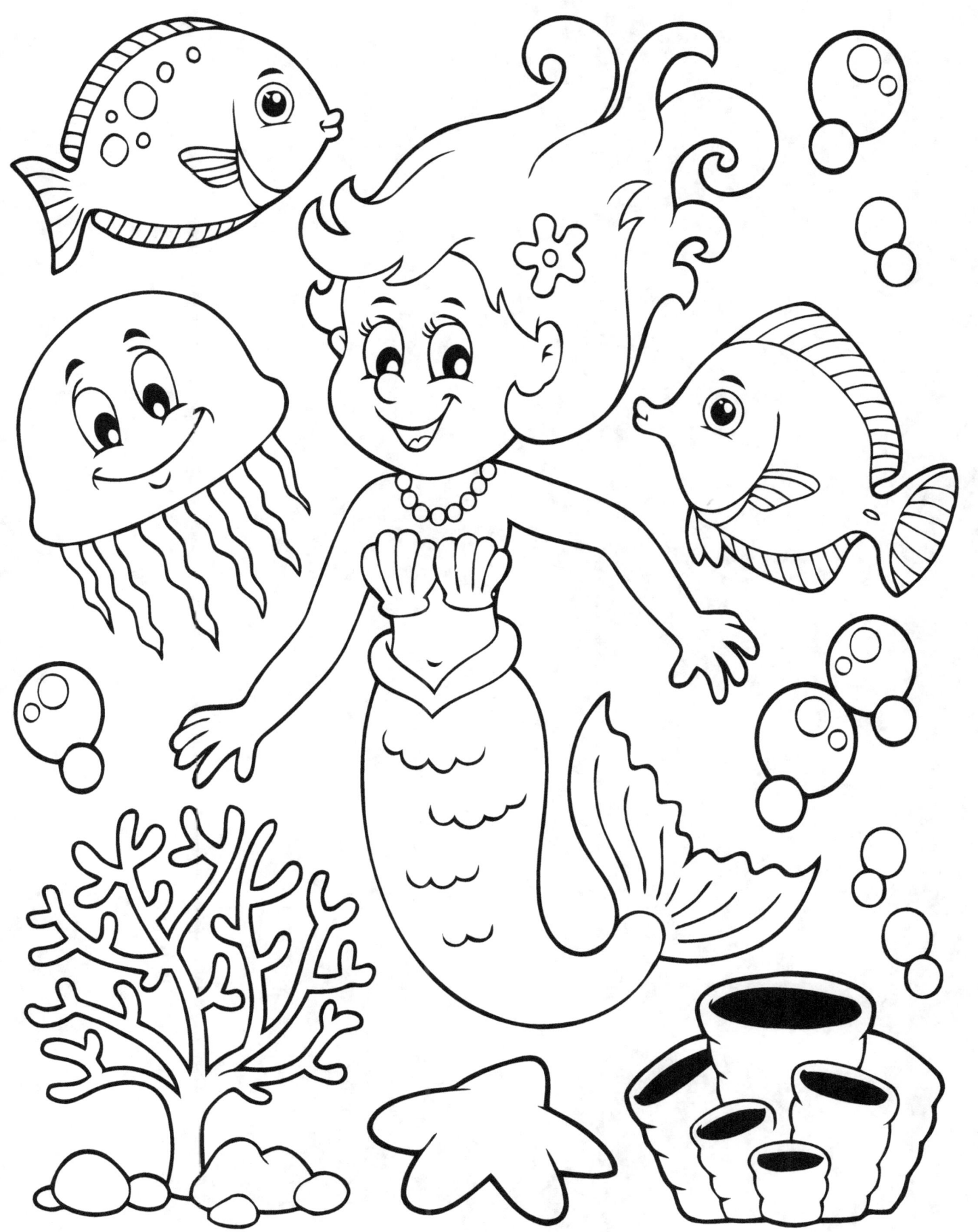

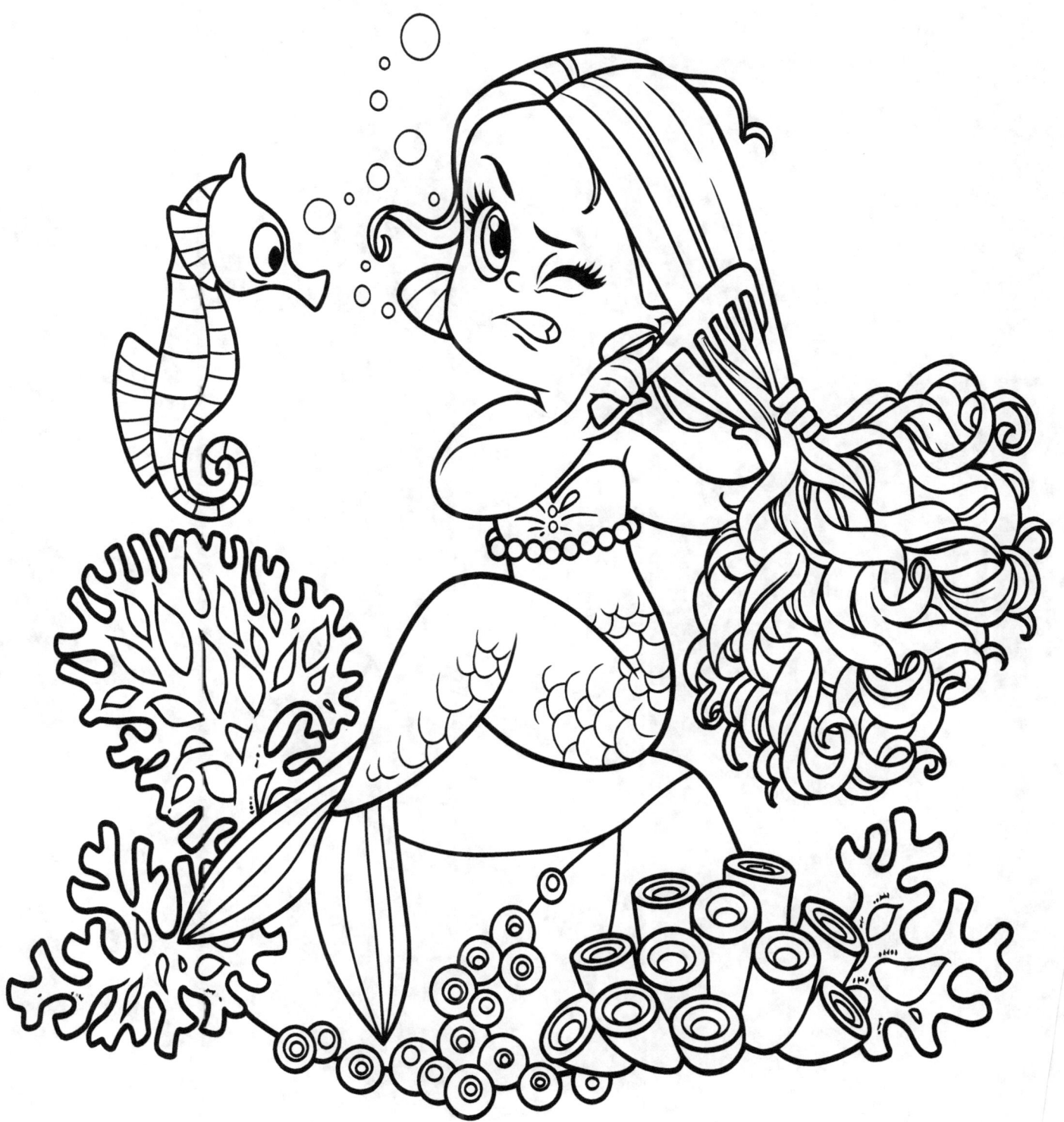

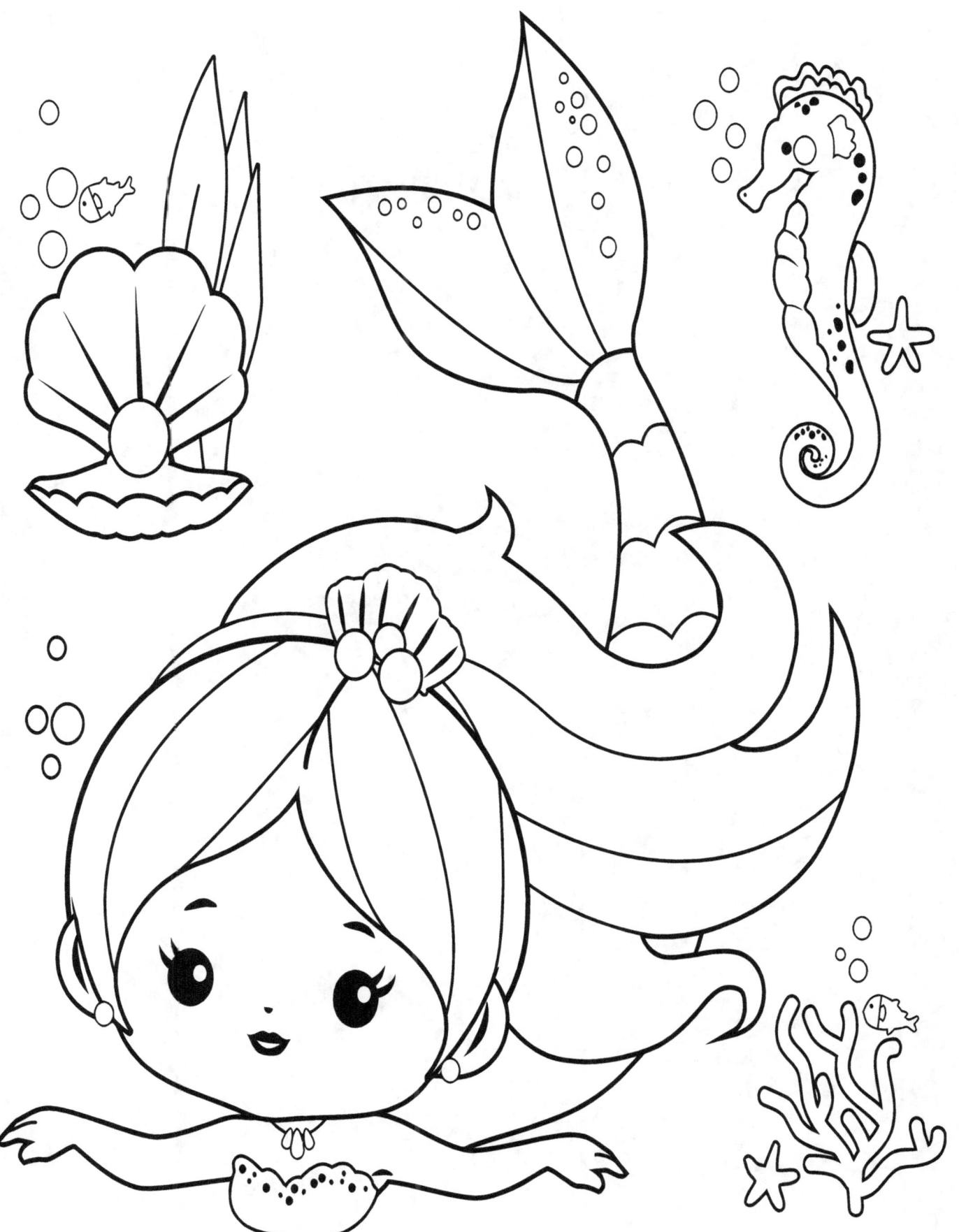

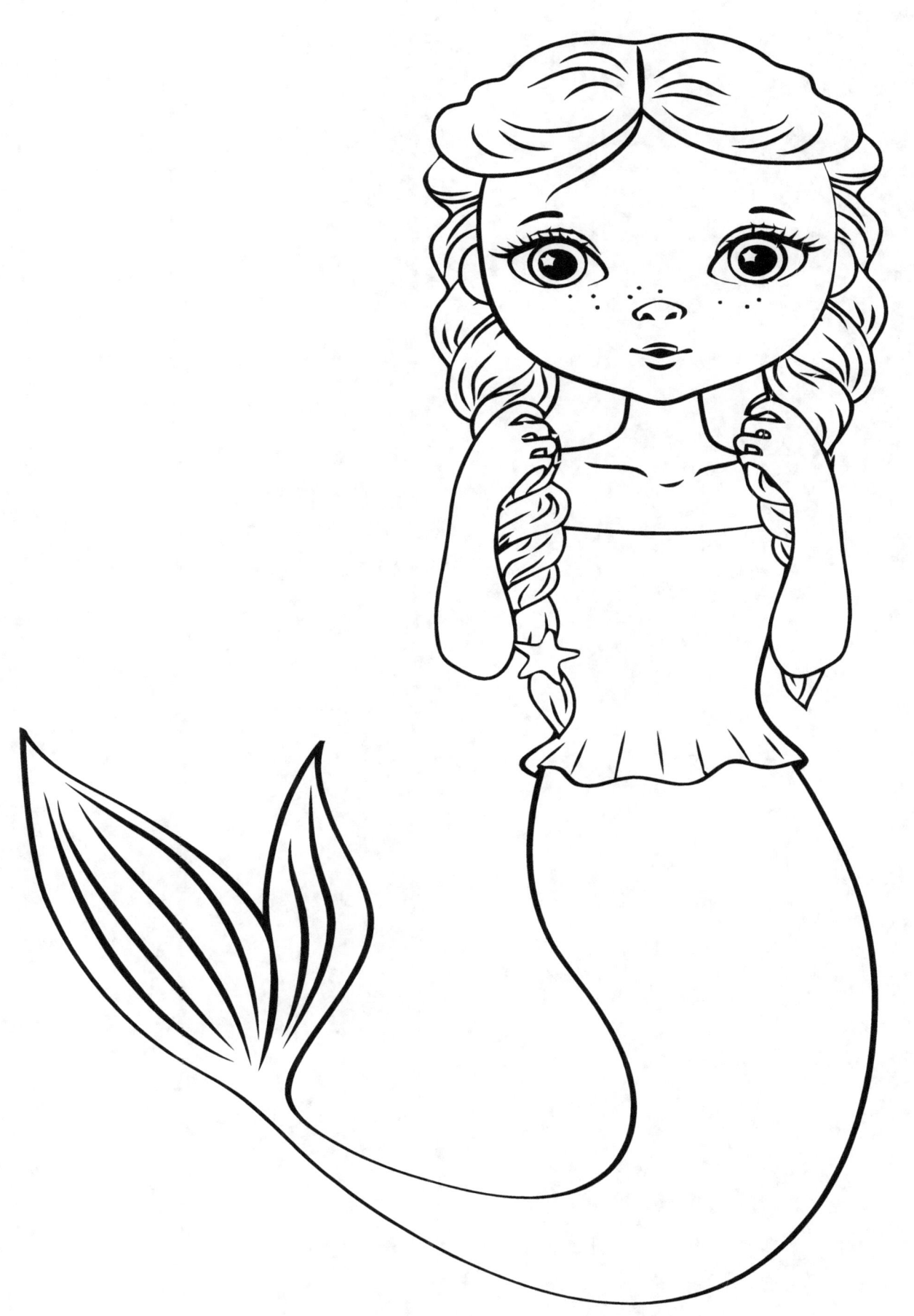

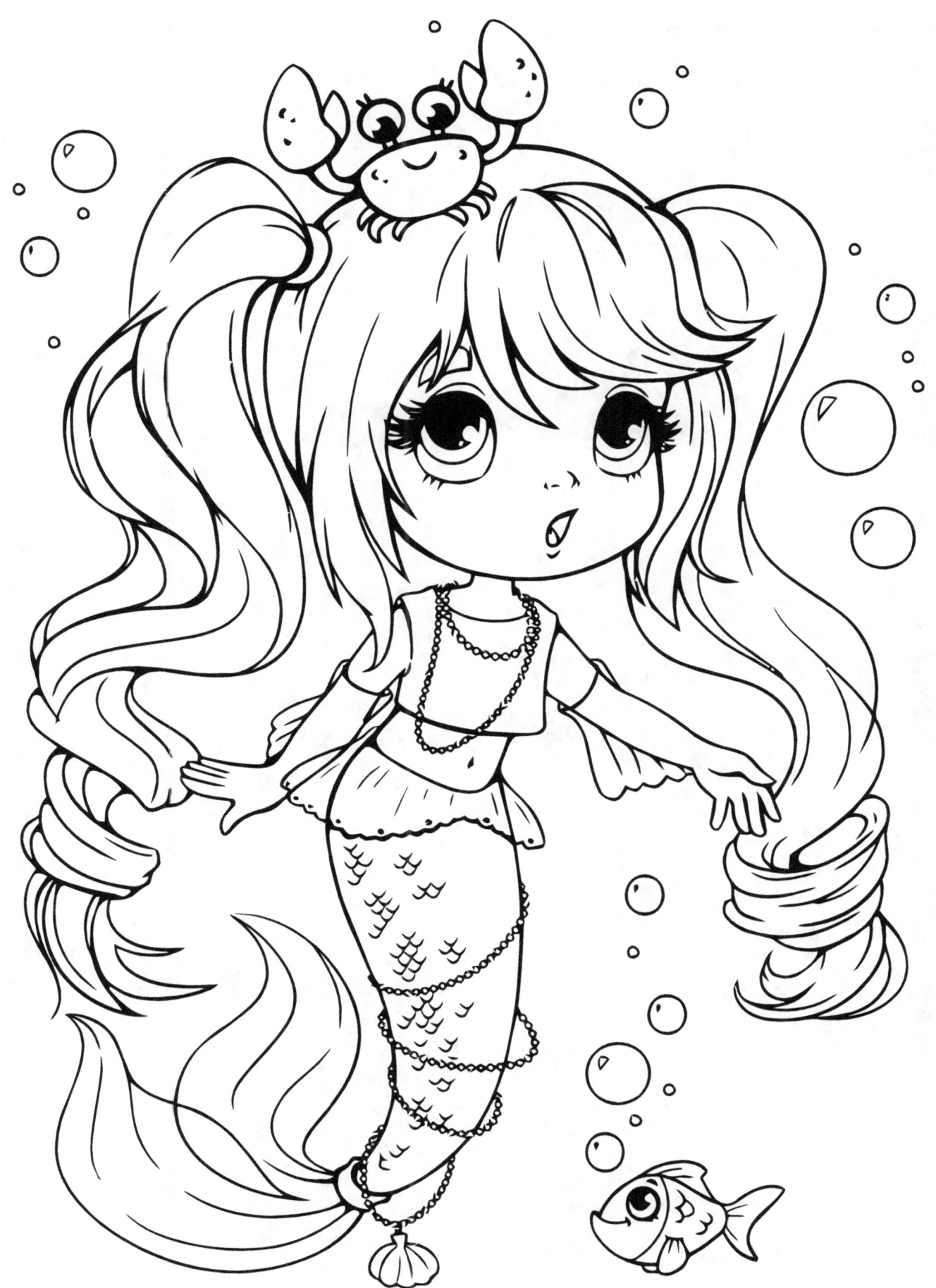

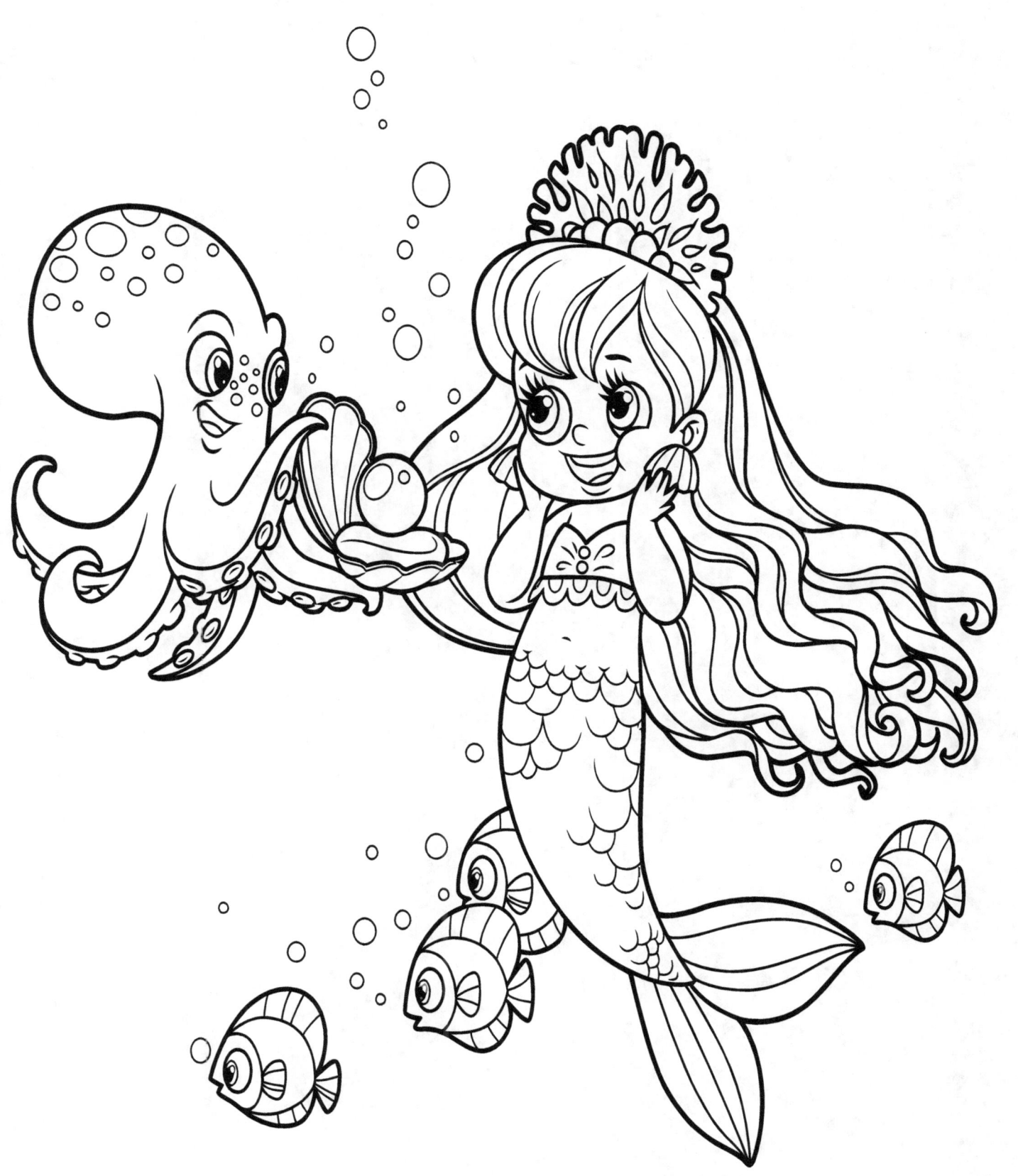

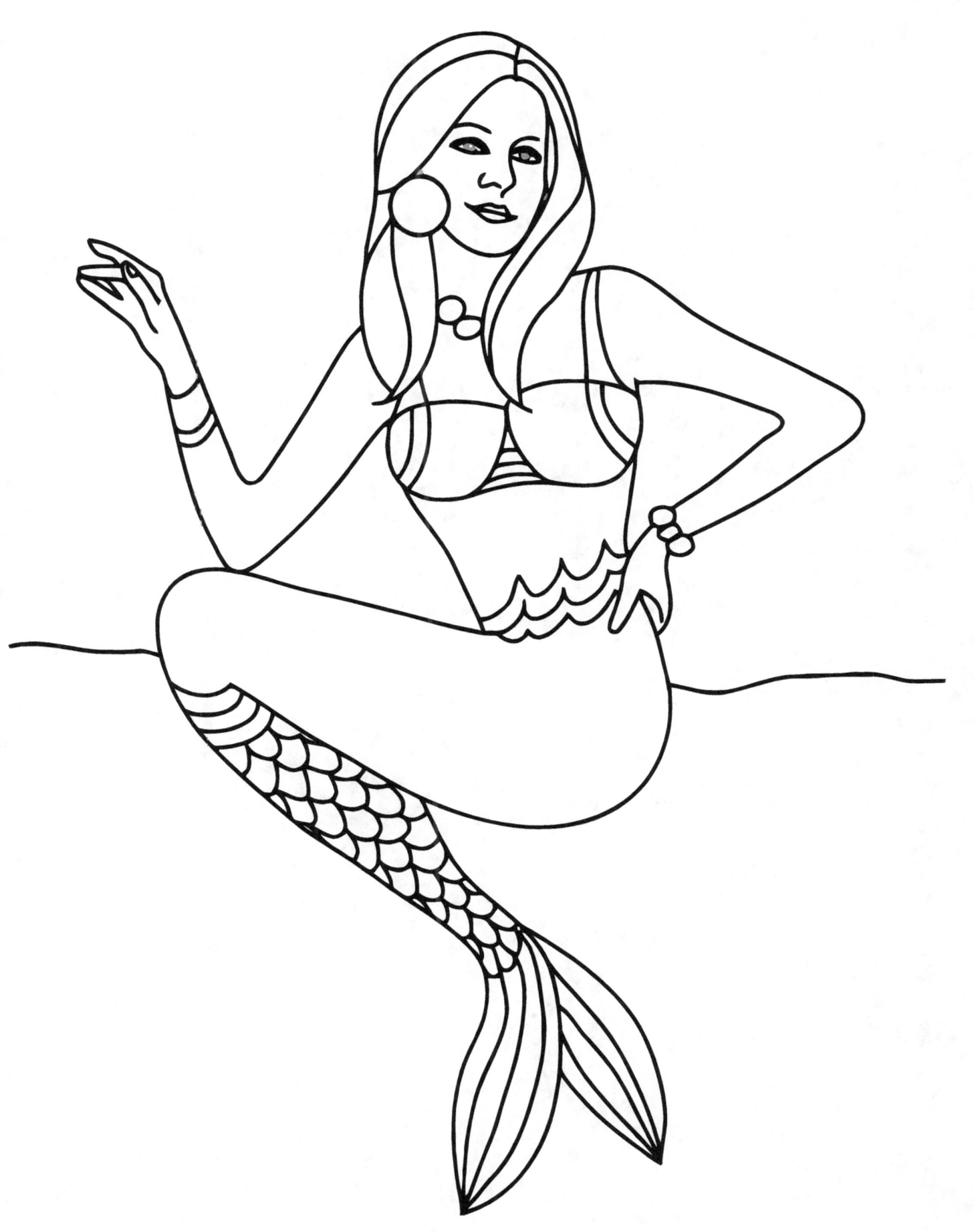

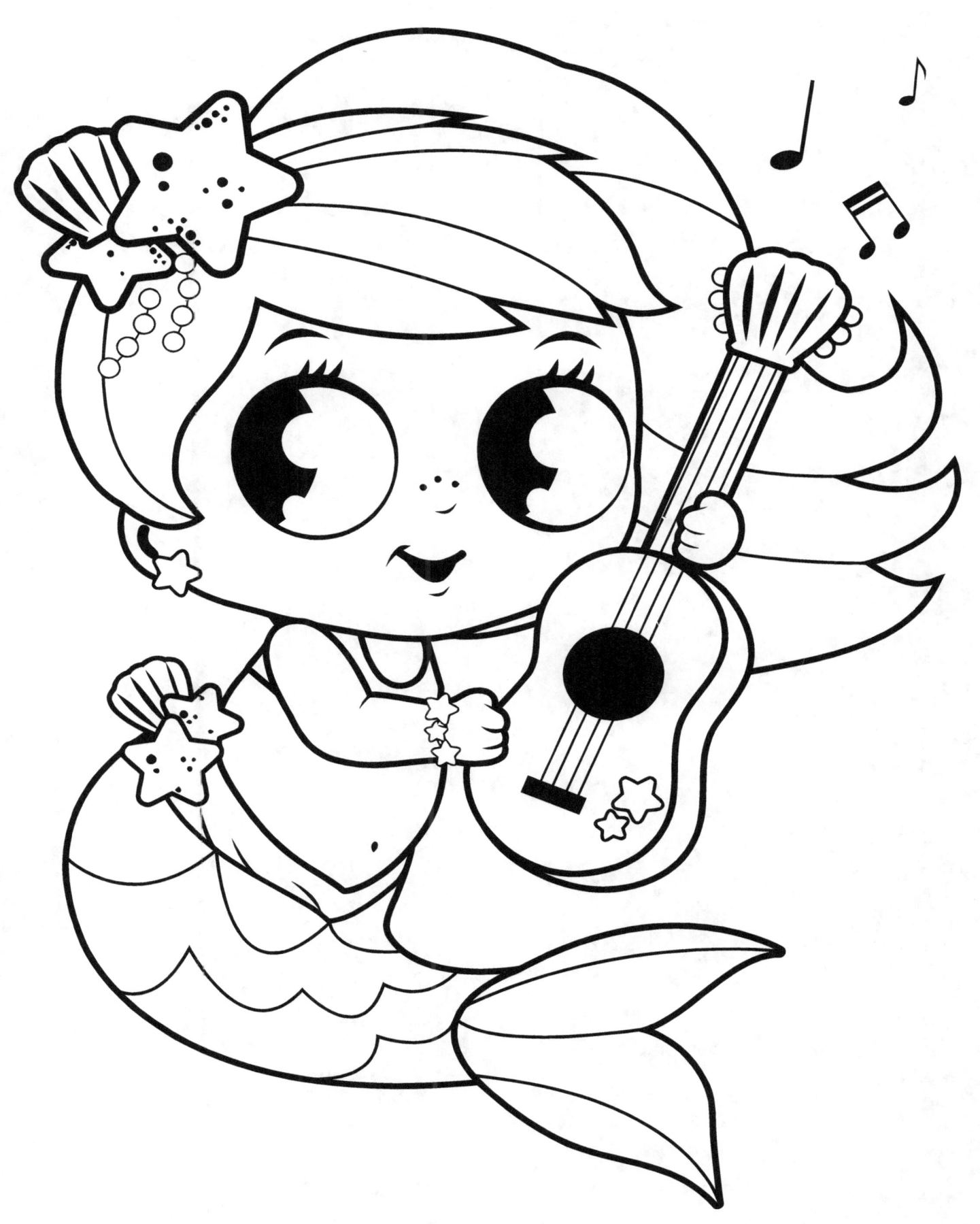

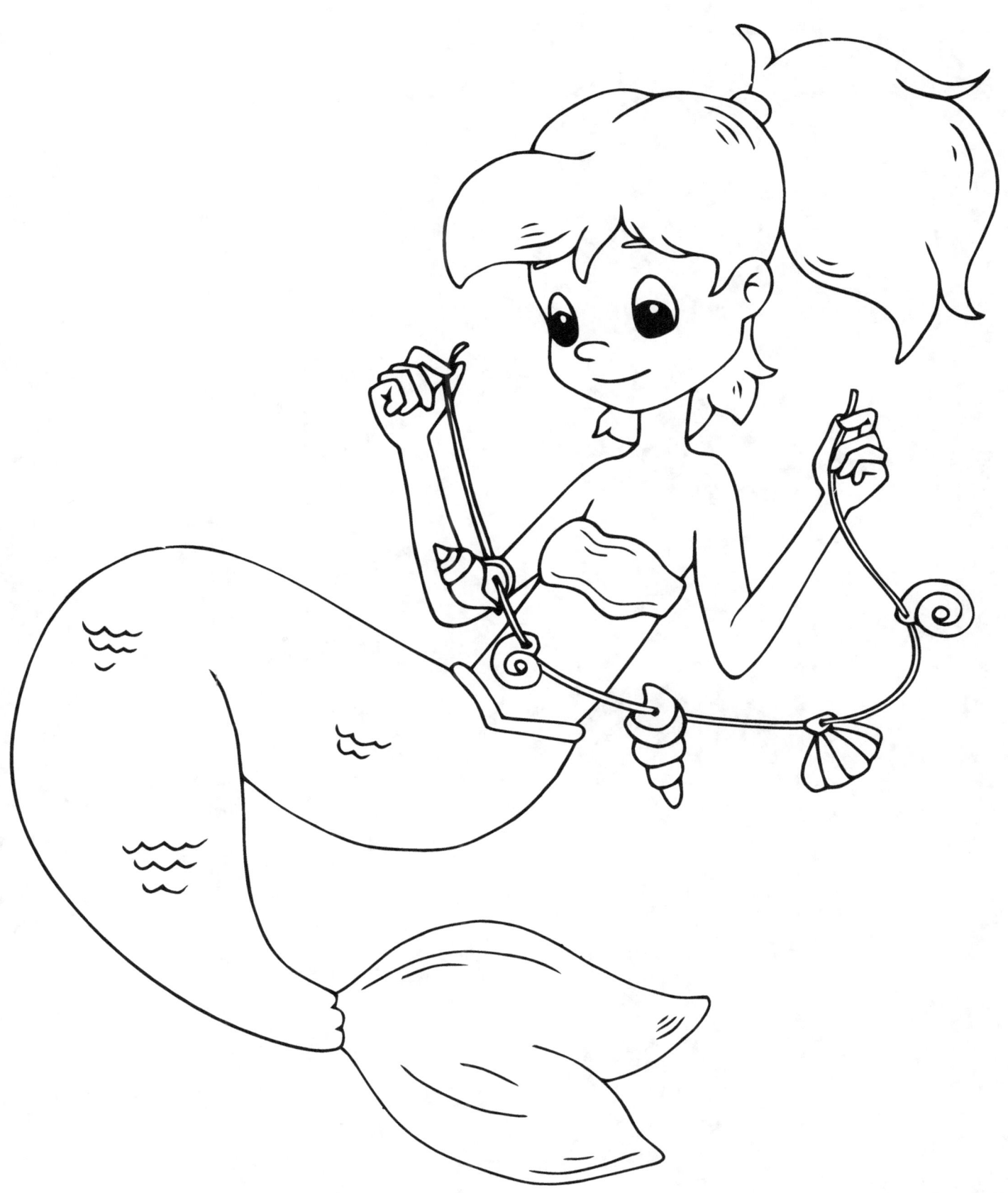

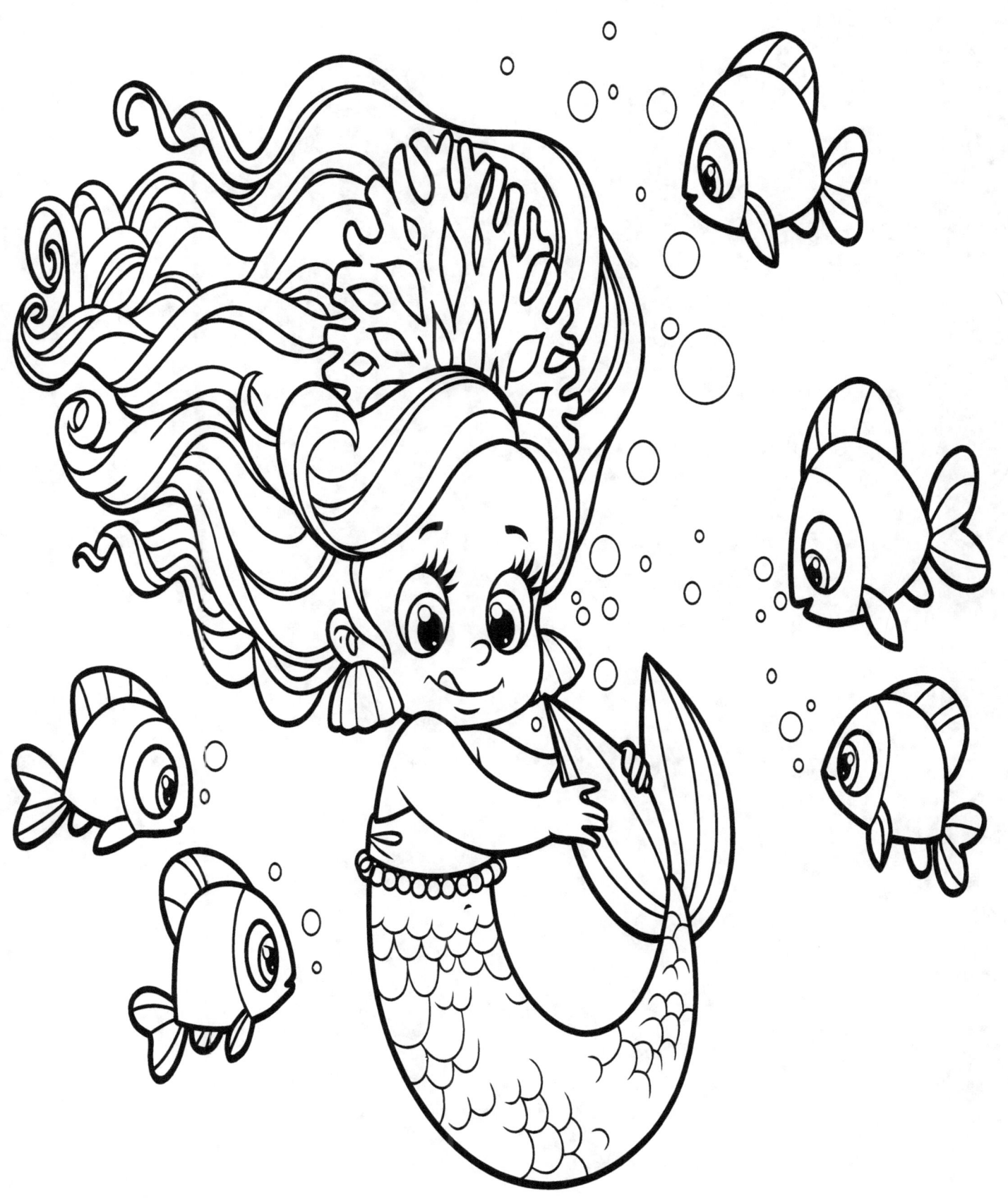

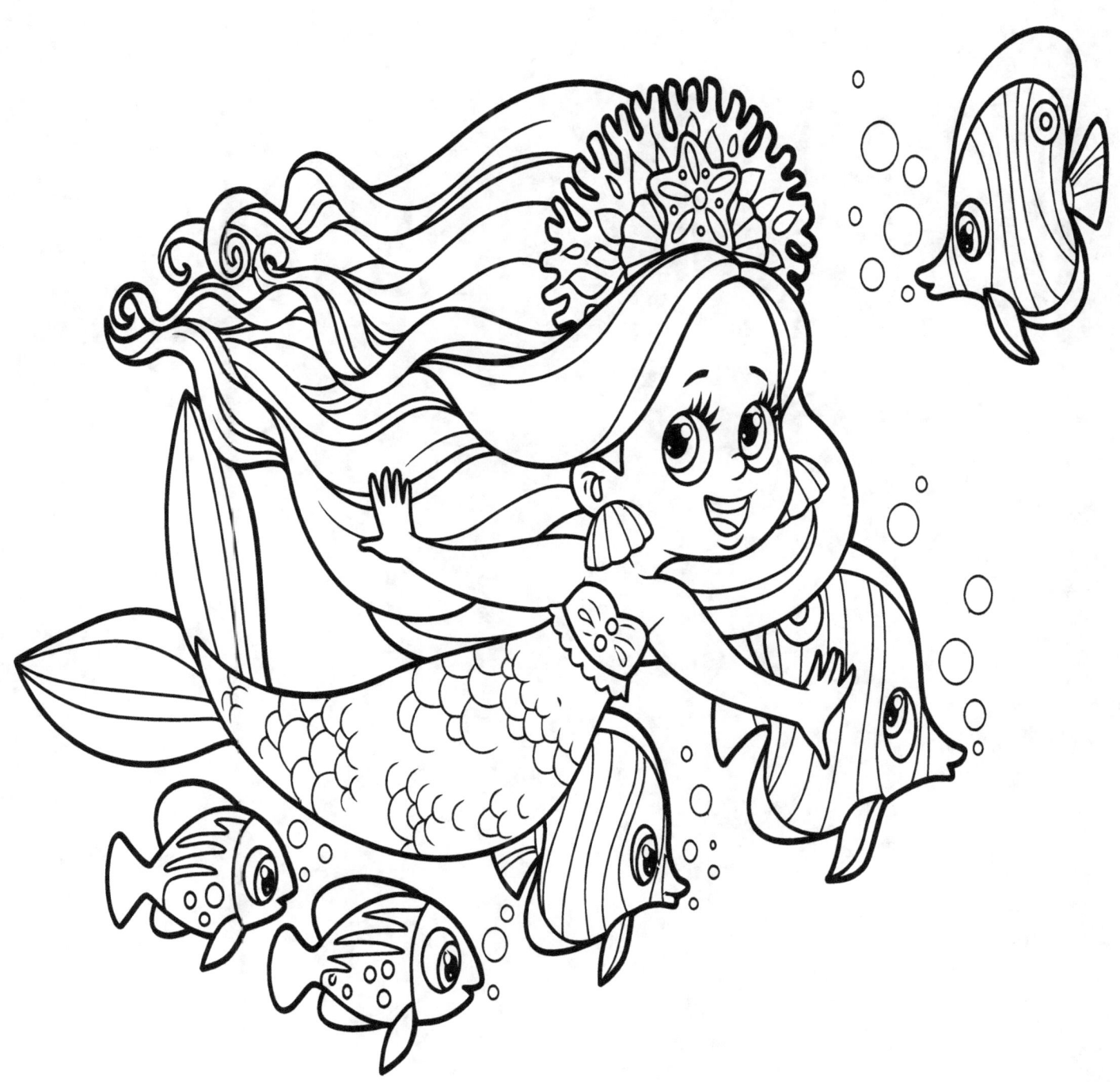

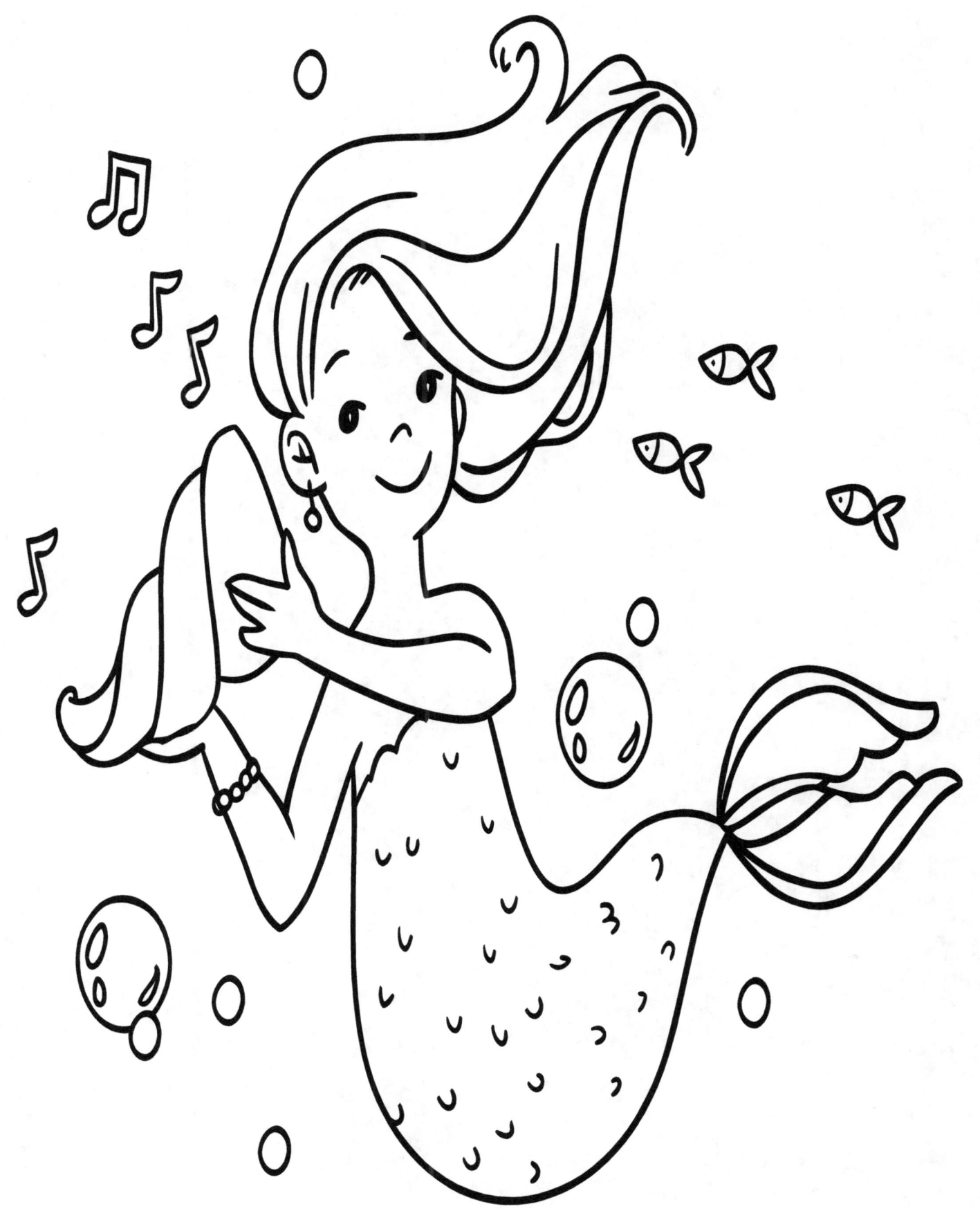

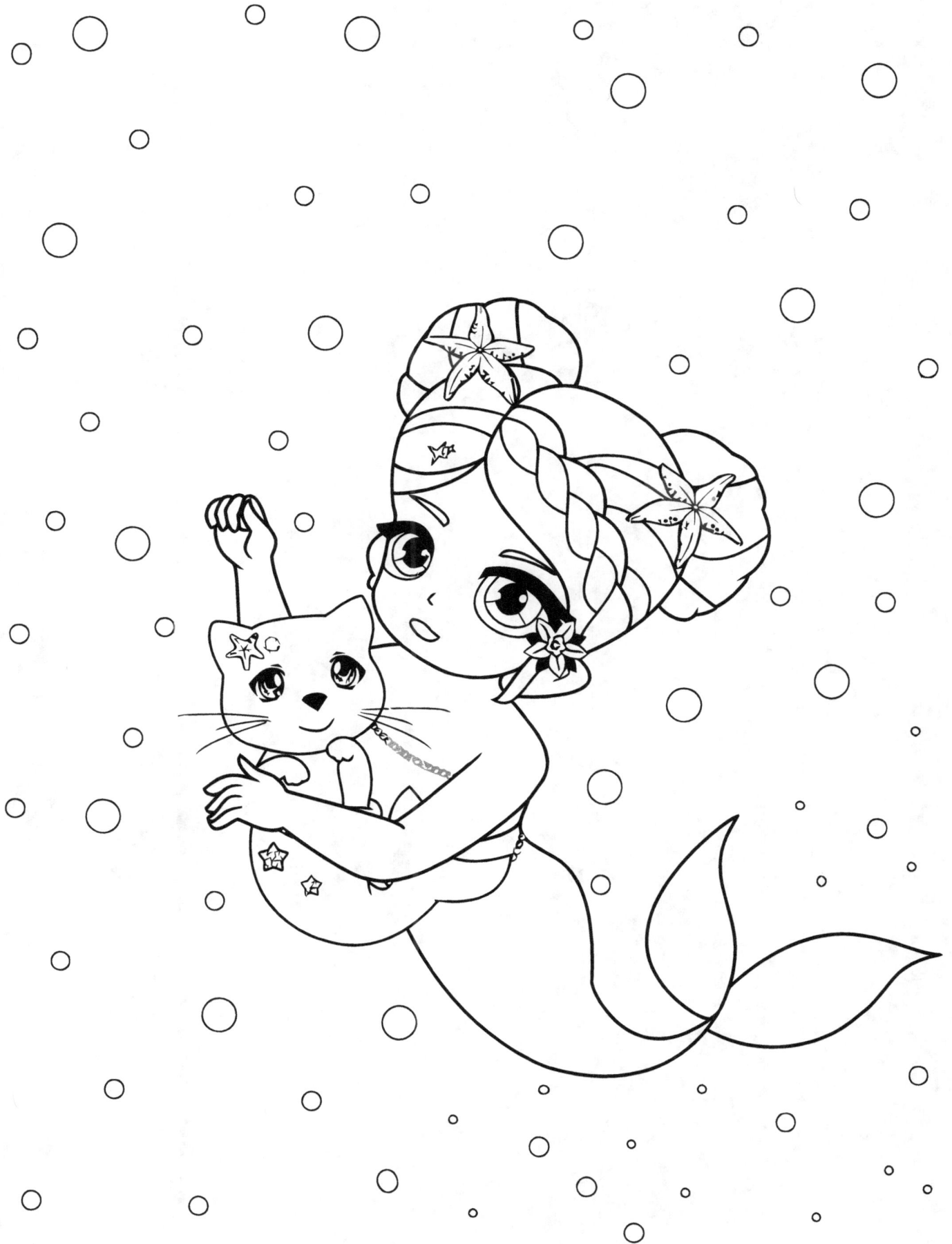

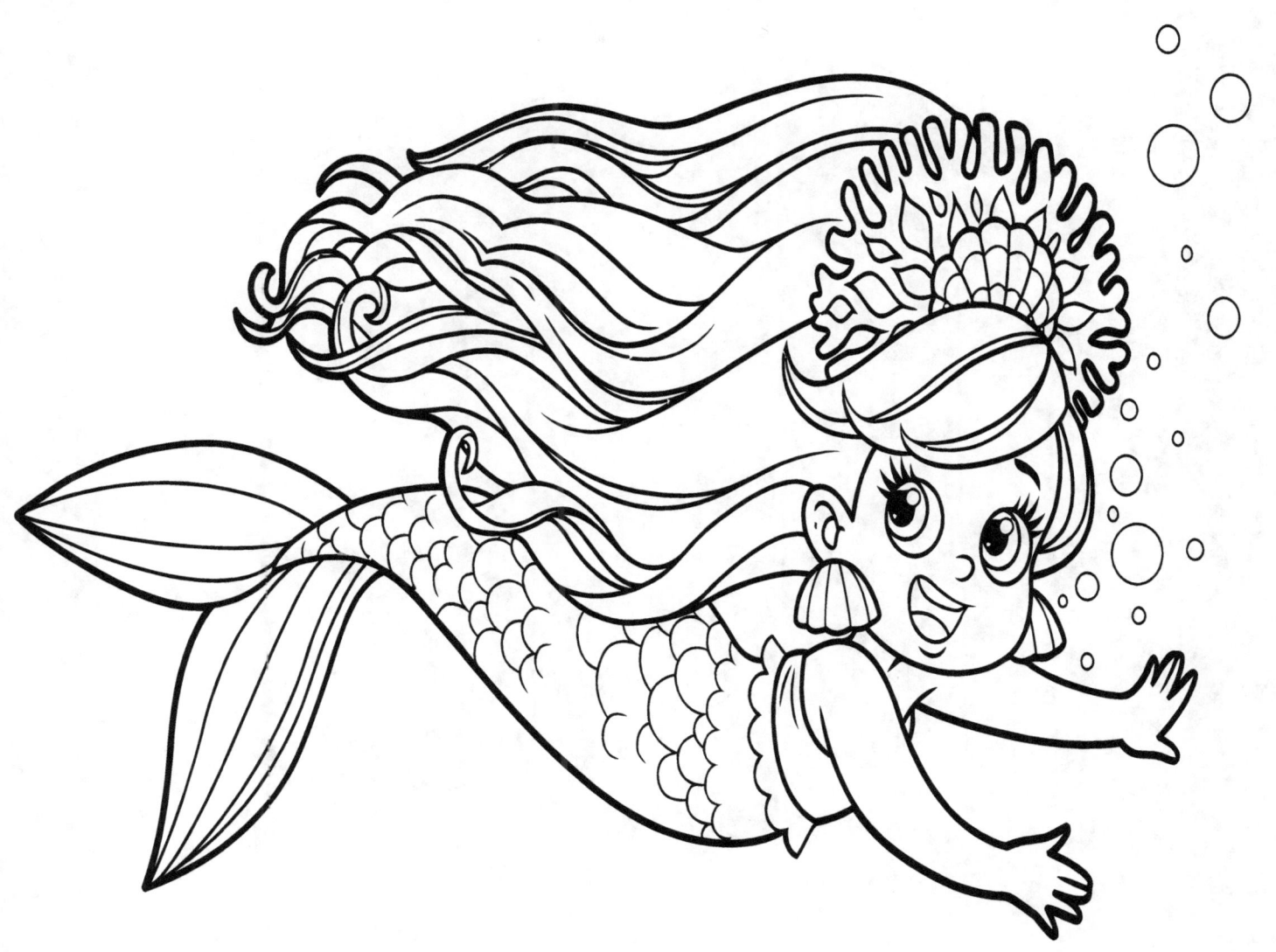

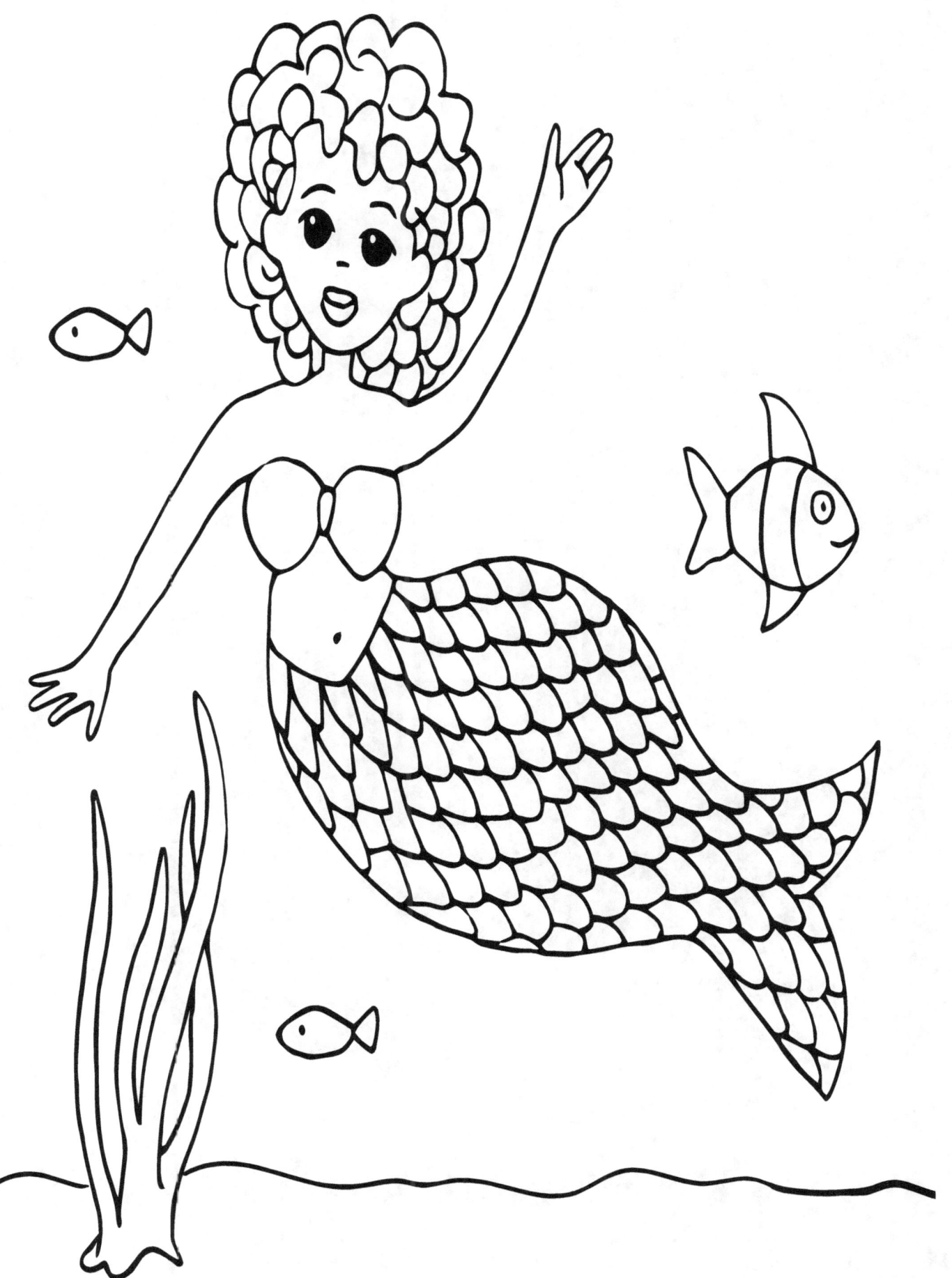

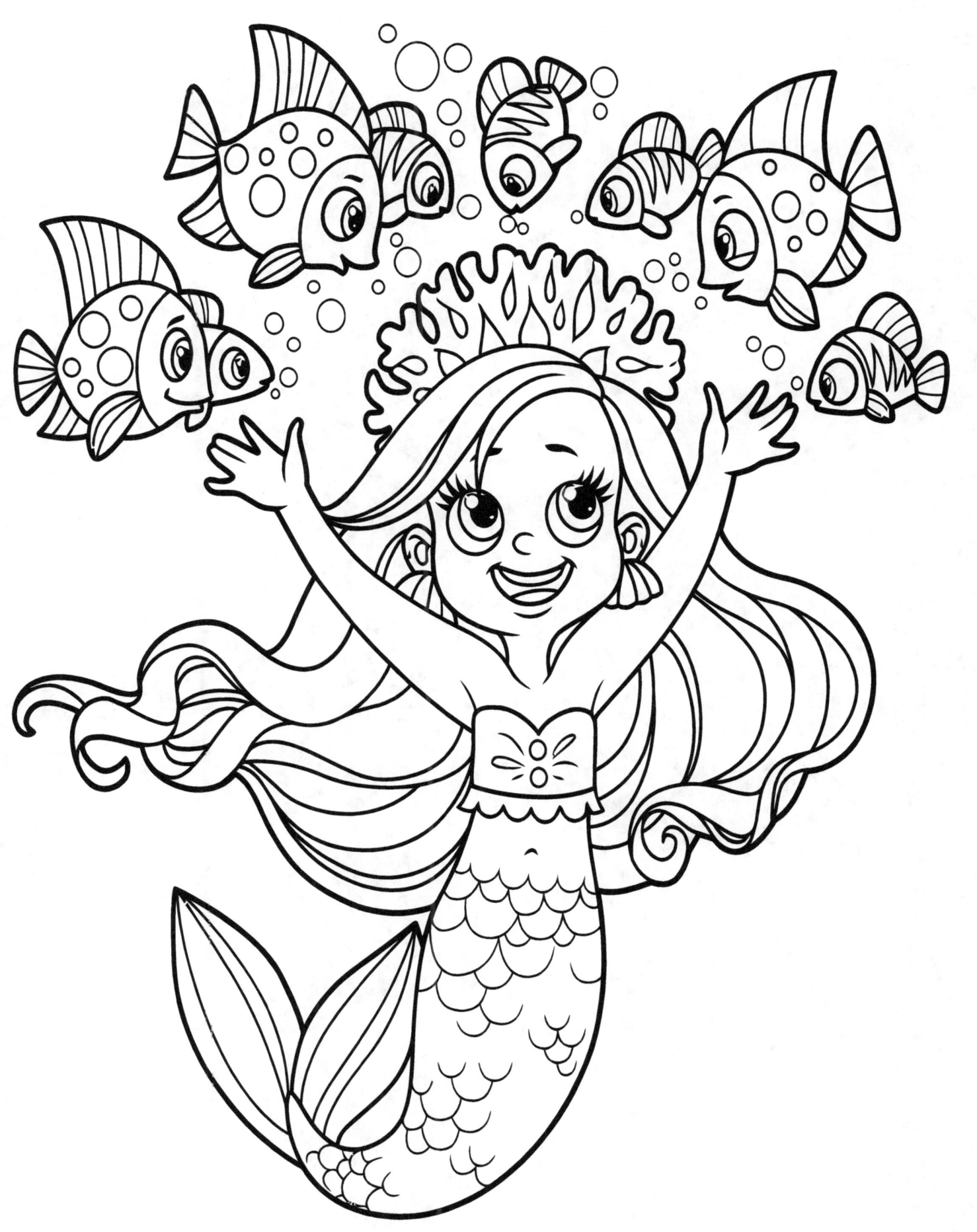

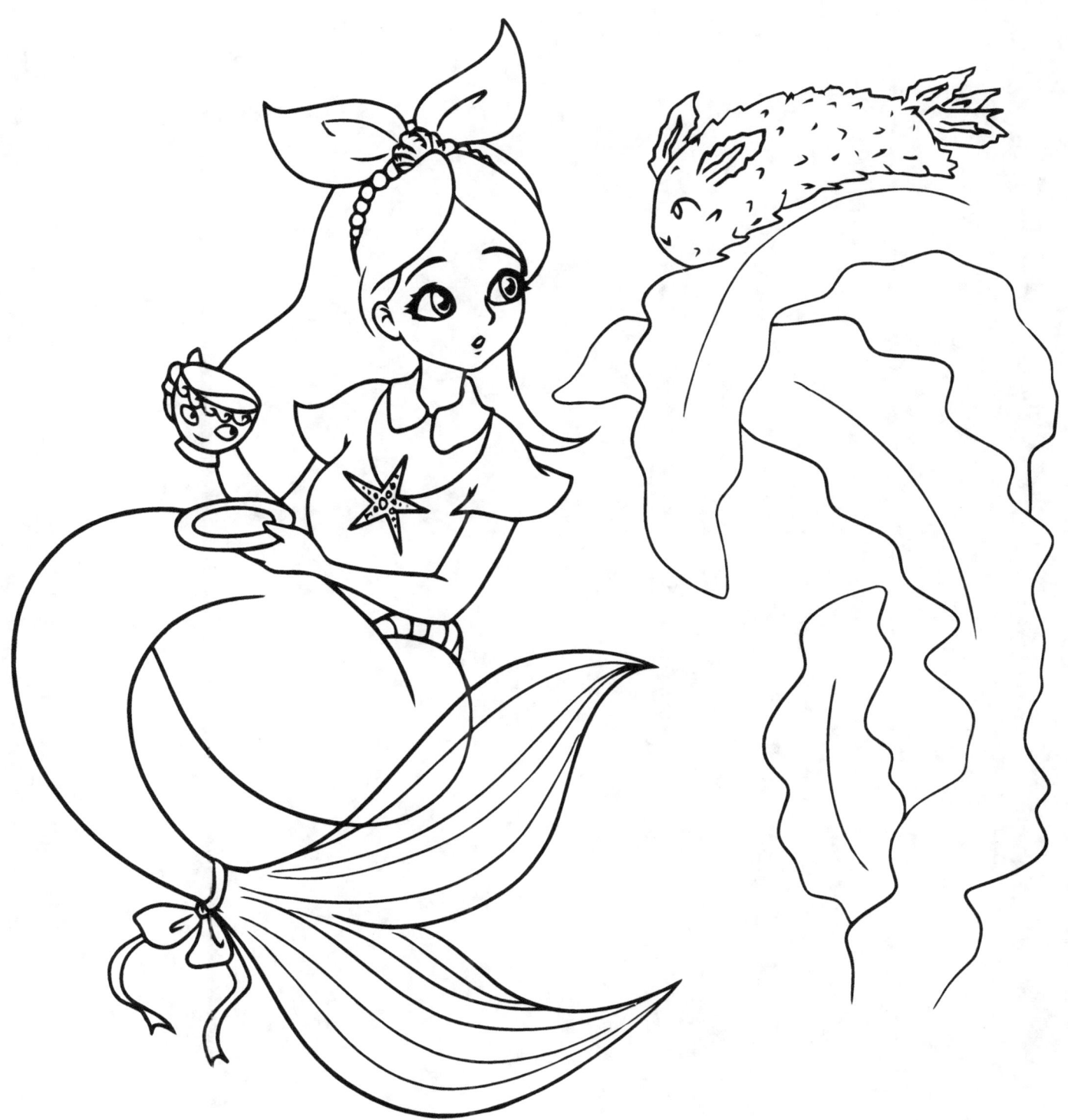

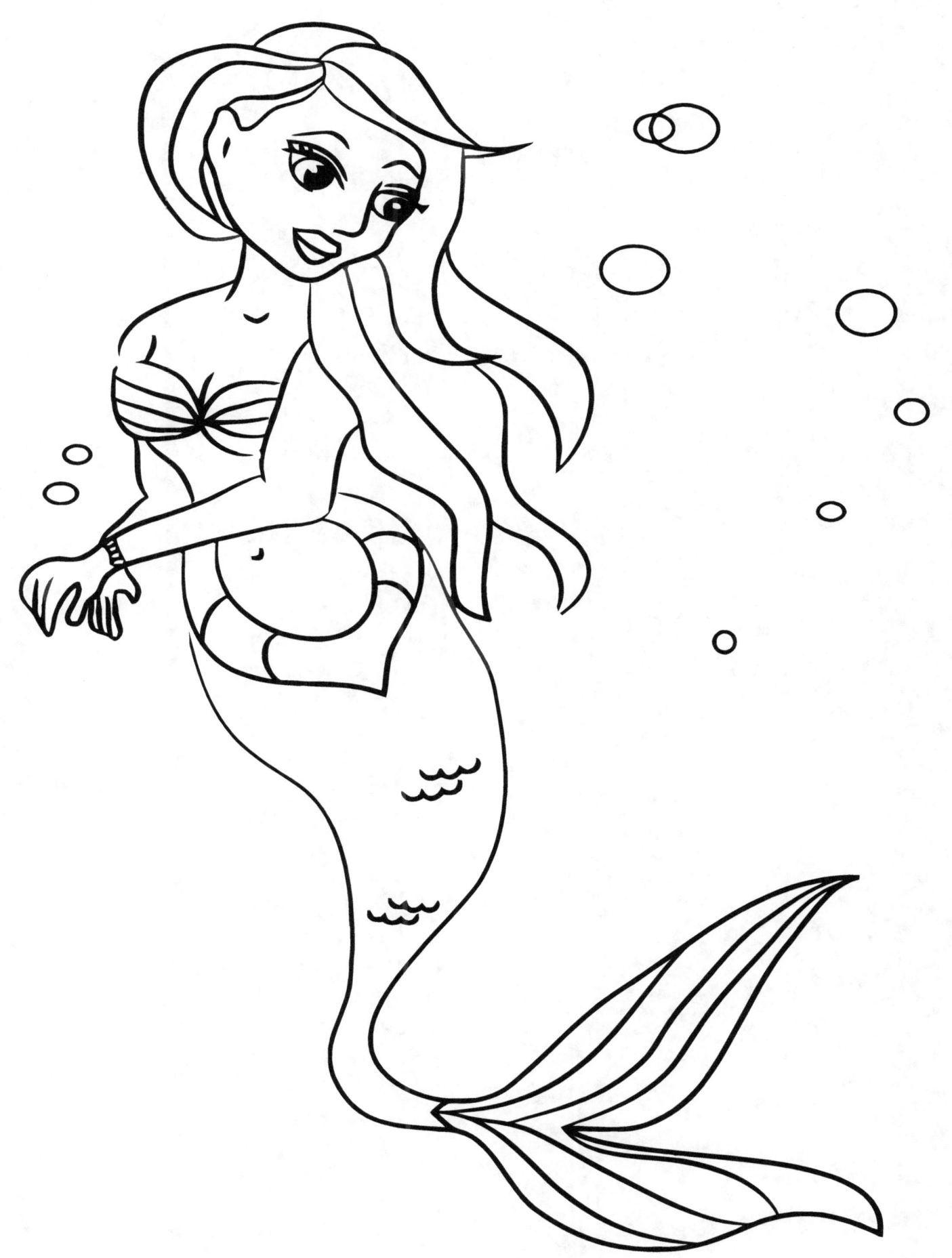

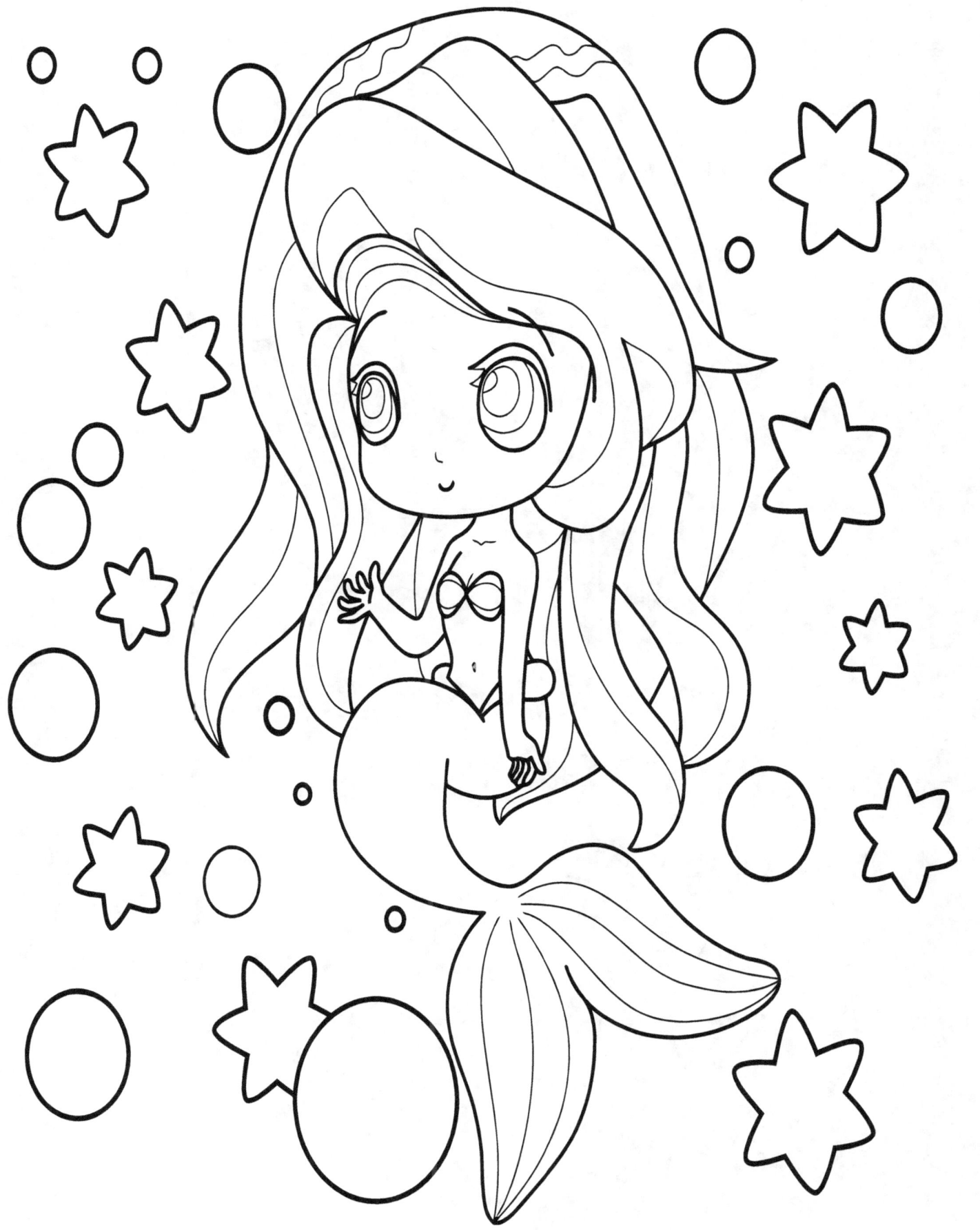

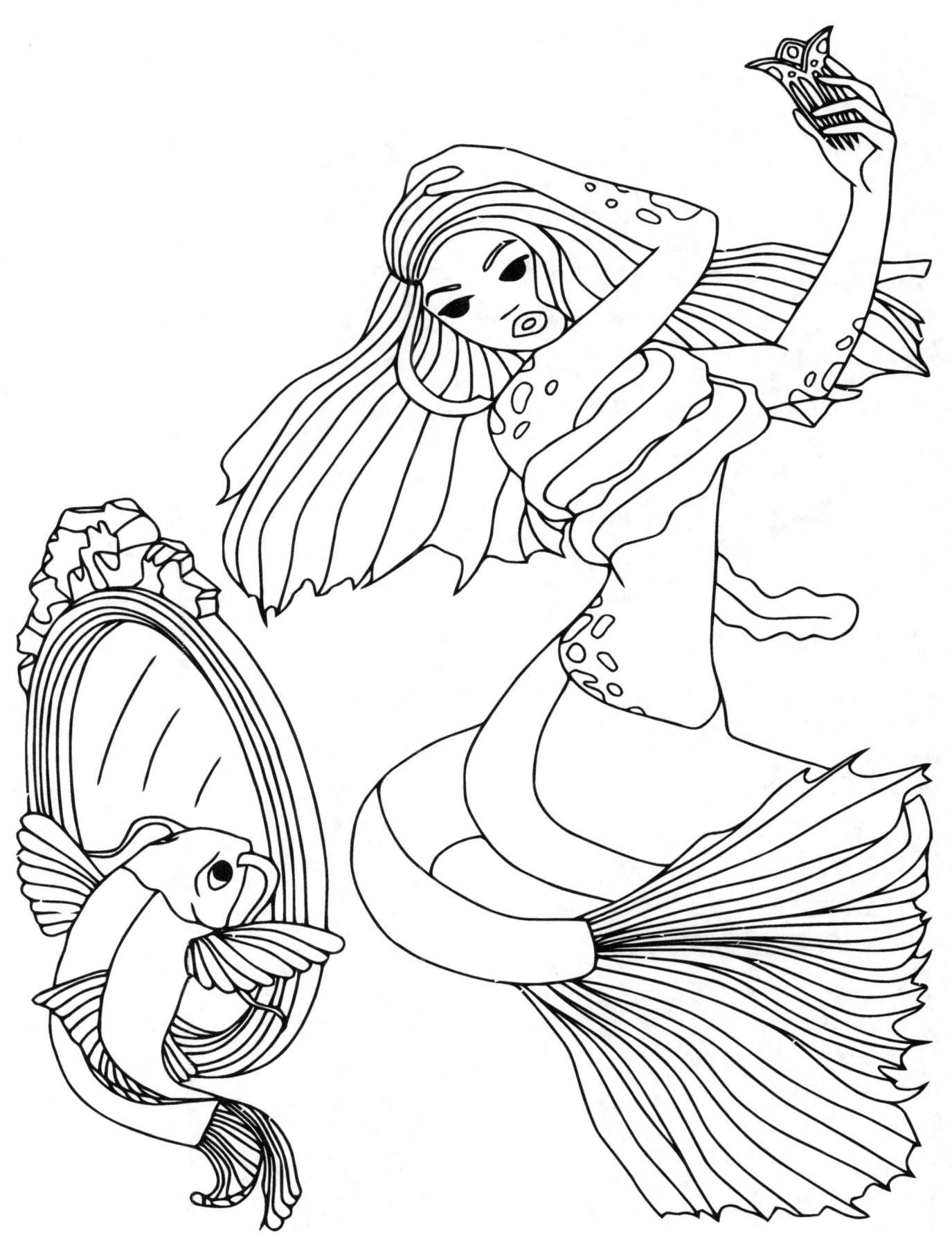

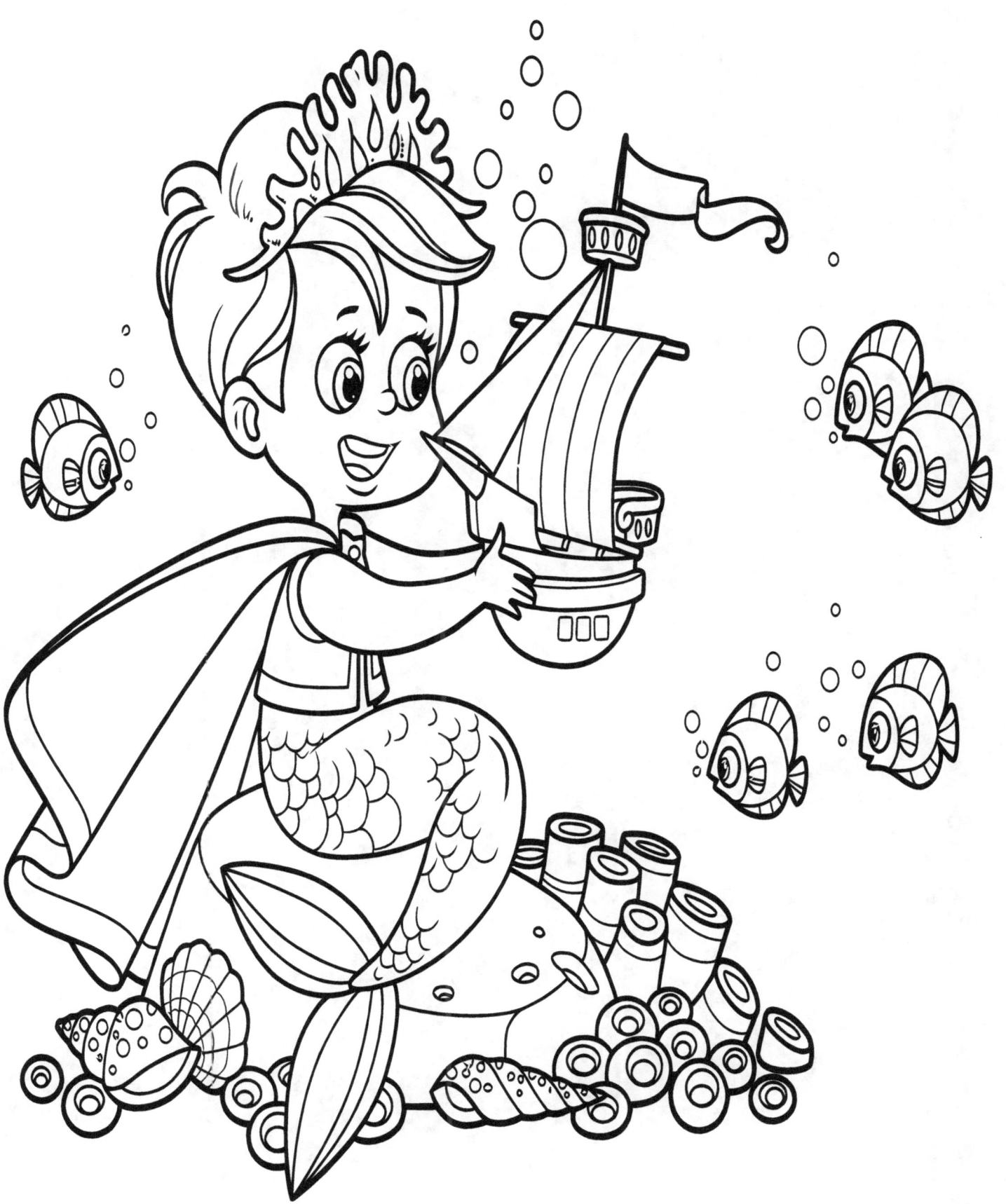

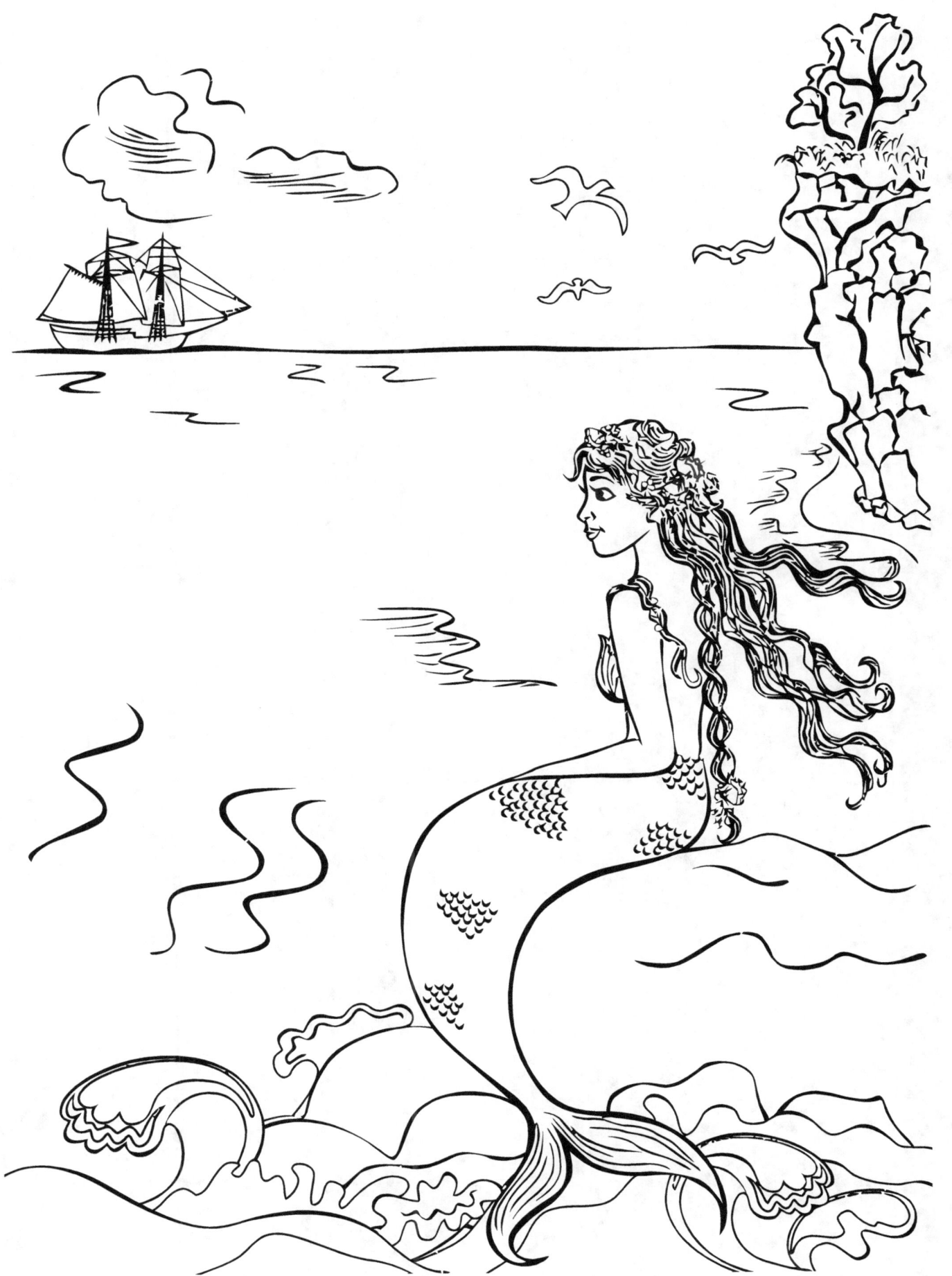

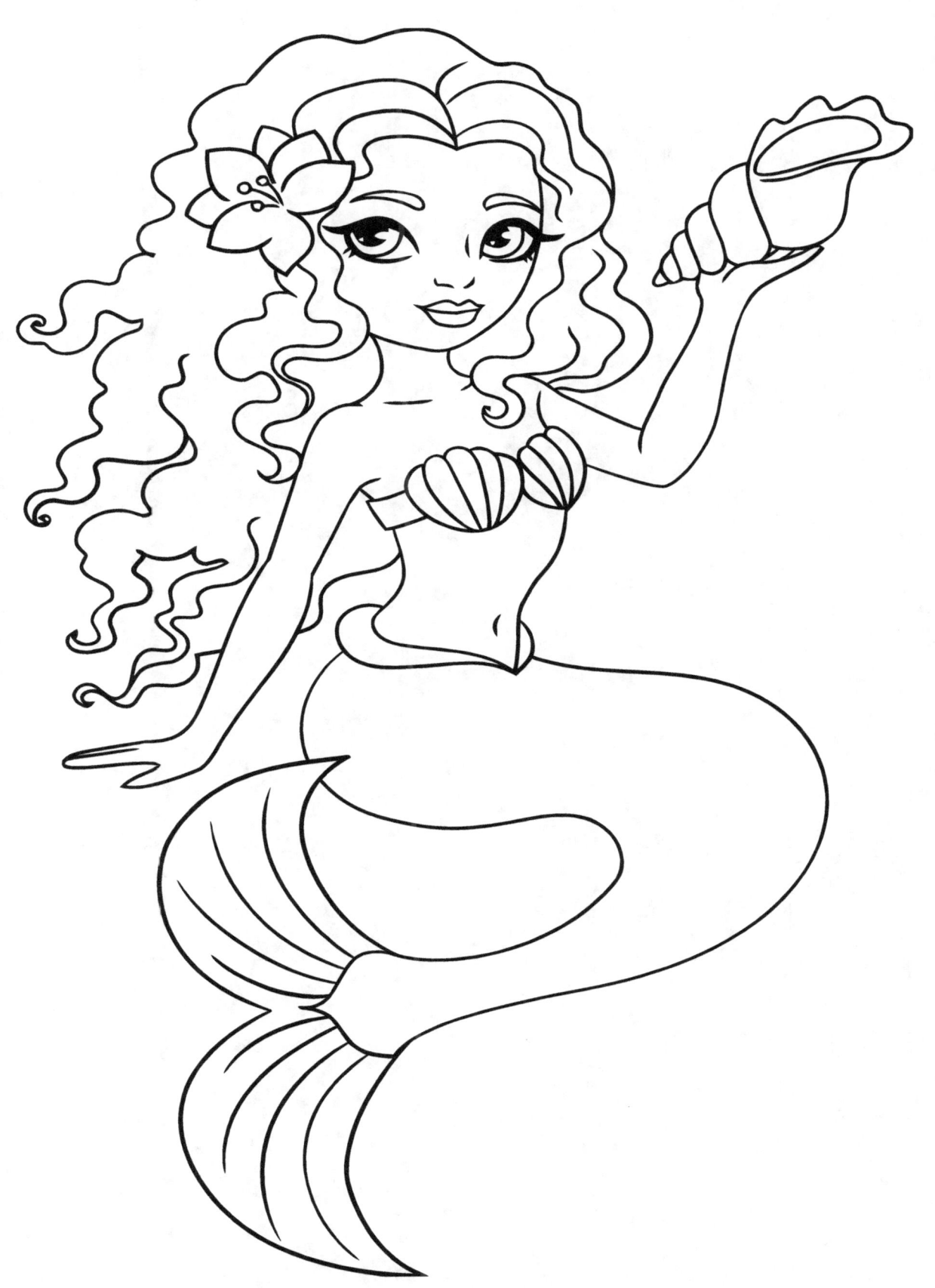

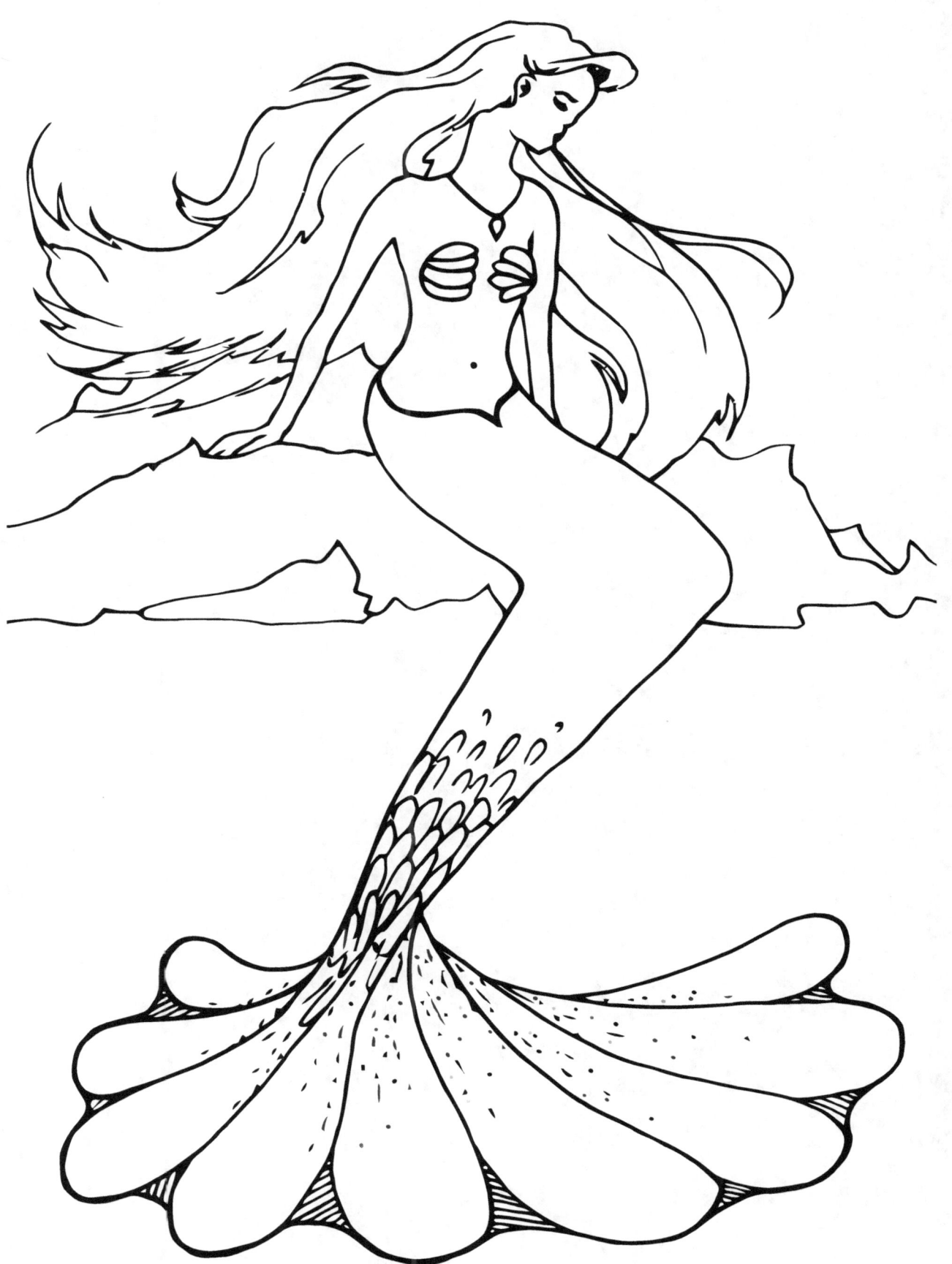

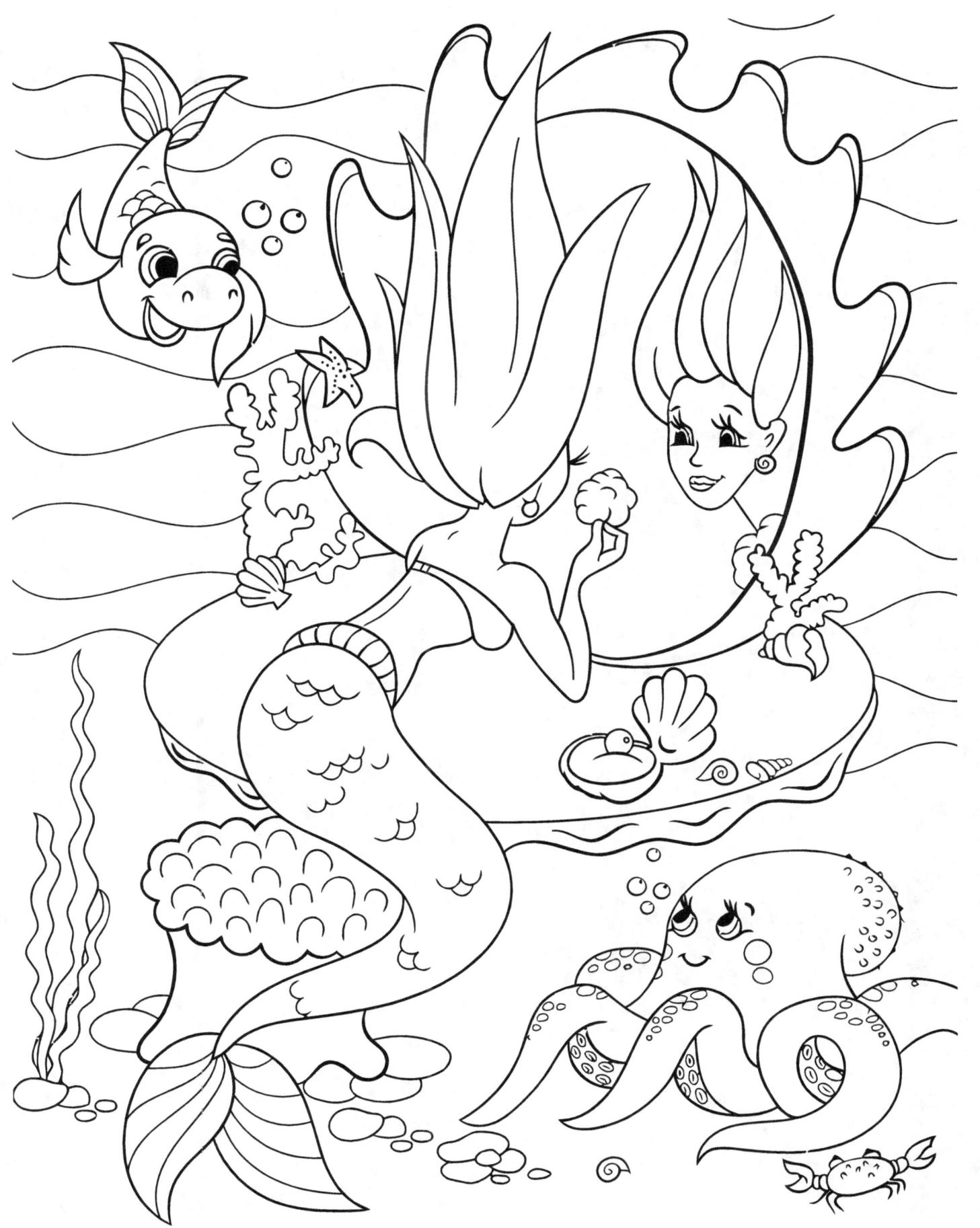

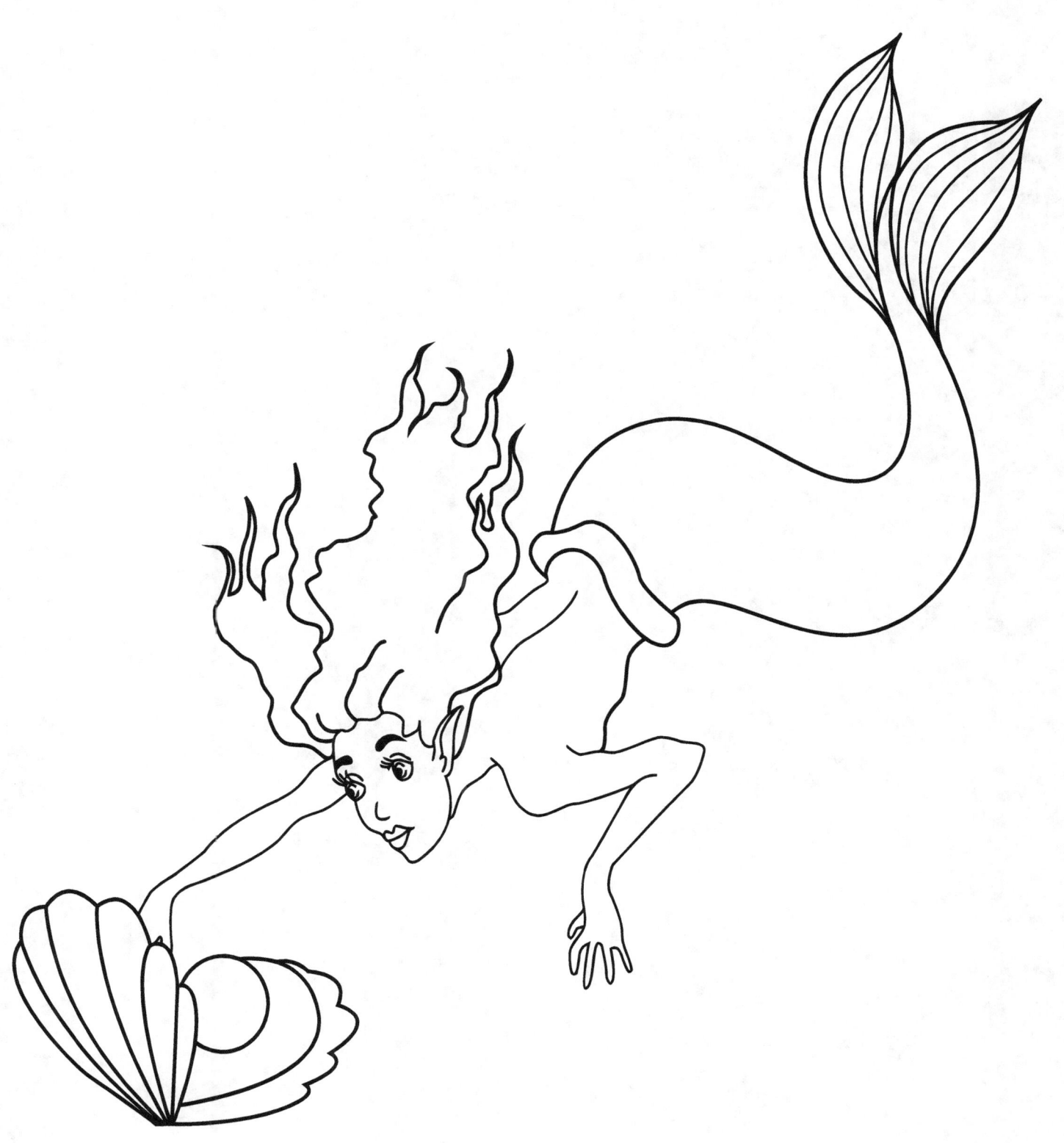